UNITT'S
BOTTLES
&
VALUES
&
MORE

REVISED UPDATED
& ENLARGED EDITION
WITH ADDED CATEGORIES

Compiled by
Peter and Barbara Sutton–Smith

Fitzhenry & Whiteside

Unitt's Bottles & Values & More

© 1999 by Fitzhenry & Whiteside

Fitzhenry & Whiteside acknowledges with thanks the support of the Government
of Canada through its Book Publishing Industry Development Program in the publication of this title.

Canadian Cataloguing in Publication Data

Sutton-Smith, Peter
  Unitt's bottles & values & more

Previous ed. by Peter Unitt and Anne Worrall.
Includes index.
ISBN 1-55041-205-1

1. Bottles – Collectors and collecting – Canada. 2. Beverage industry – Collectibles
– Prices – Canada. I. Unitt, Peter, 1914- . Unitt's bottles & values & more. II Title.
III Title: Bottles & values & more. IV Tittle: Unitt's bottles and values and more

NK5440.B6U65 1999   748.8'2'0971075   C99-930100-4

Design: Darrell McCalla
Printed and Bound in Canada

Introduction

The popularity of the bottle as a collectable is not hard to understand. A small collection can be started quite easily, children and adults can share in the hunt and although rare items can be bought, sometimes it is possible to find them while digging or hidden in cellars, attics and old buildings.

In downtown Toronto when land was being excavated for the Convention Centre and then later for the Dome Stadium, many treasures were discovered from bygone eras. And as more lands are presently being developed collectors are again on the lookout.

During the summer months scuba divers enjoy themselves on the Muskoka Lakes following the routes of the old pleasure boats for mineral and pop bottles thrown overboard by tourists.

Every Province and areas have their known hunting grounds, and when a new source is discovered it's amazing how word gets around and collectors arrive for the search like "bees round a honey pot."

Also don't give up on your local markets and thrift stores. A small-size sealed bottle made in England, 4 inches wide and 5 inches tall, with a seal marked with the raised letters "CP" and the date 1697 was reported recently to have been purchased in a Florida thrift store for $5, and later sold by Norman Heckler & Company for $9,900.

For those who wish to make a collection of bottles with a Canadian background the choice is large and unless only rare bottles appeal the collection will grow quickly. Selecting from the wider area of bottles made in North America and Europe there are more types of bottles and almost infinite variety. Specializing in a certain type of bottle is never easy and takes travel, time and money. The prices of the rarer bottles attest to this.

Collectors are always seeking information, realizing that knowledge is an aid to enjoyment and an essential tool for acquiring a good collection. As the title suggests this book contains information about bottles and their history as well as their prices. To assist the collector we have included sections about bottle making; lips and closures; factories and their trade marks.

Meeting other people with similar interests is an important aspect of any hobby and the bottle collectors are fortunate in this regard. It is quite easy to find other collectors at one of the "Nostalgia" or "Bottle" shows which are being held successfully at an increasing number of locations. Also bottle clubs have been in existence for some time and usually welcome new members. Many collectors specialize and are very knowledgeable in their own field, often sharing the expertise they have acquired with others. A good way to find out about clubs is to go to one of the shows and ask around: the collectors and dealers are friendly folk and are usually pleased to help.

See Acknowledgements on page 296

Front Cover Photograph
(Courtesy of NSA Auctions, Cambridge, Ontario.)

Back row:
POISON BOTTLE EMBOSSED AND LABELLED
"POISON/ – / USE WITH CAUTION." Cobalt blue irregular hexagon. Tooled flanged lip, 8 oz size, base embossed with "D" in a diamond. Label "CARBOLIC ACID," logo of skull and cross bones, "C ALAN HOBLEY WALKERTON ONT." Label is beige with red text, some wear. 6 3/4" x 2 3/8" x 1 7/8". **$53**

SODA BOTTLE
"ROBERTSON & BROOKS, MOUNT FOREST". Quart size in amber with applied crown. **$265**

RARE SODA BOTTLE
"VICTORIA/SODA WATER WORKS/ logo of crossed swords/REGISTERED" other side "MB FAUGHNER/MEAFORD ONT." Blop top, squat soda in deep aqua. Not many examples of this bottle. 7 3/8" x 2 1/2". **$150**

Front row:
CERAMIC INK WELL
White with painted decoration in green, gold, blue, purple and red. Square with beveled corners. No lid. European 1860 - 1880. size 2" x 2" x 2". **$33**

POISON BOTTLE
"POISON/POISON" on sides. Deep honey amber, tooled lip, rectangular with raised diamonds on sides/corners. Minor external/internal flaws. 1 1/4" x 4 3/8". **$40**

LABELLED AND EMBOSSED INK
"FF/DALLEY & CO/HAMILTON". Aqua, house shaped, tooled lip. Label reads, "DALLEYS/FINE/VIOLET/INK/ FF DALLEY & CO/HAMILTON ONT." Label is pale green with red, black & beige. Not often found with label. 1 3/8" x 1 3/8" x 2 3/4". **$120**

CERAMIC INK WELL
"Delft" blue. Blue and white with two scenes of ships and two of flowers. Corners form feet. European 1860-1880. 2 1/4" x 2 1/4" x 1 7/8". **$90**

Contents

Avon

Originally the California Perfume Company, formed in 1886. The Avon name was used from 1929 and became Avon Products Inc. in 1939.

The attractive containers, packages and awards of Avon Products Inc. are a popular collectable in Canada and the United States.

"55 THUNDERBIRD" (1975-76)
After shave. Blue glass with plastic cap. 2 oz. With box. **$14**

"56 TRIUMPH TR3" (1975-76)
After shave. Blue/green glass, plastic cap. 2 oz. With box. **$15**

"1936 M G DECANTER" (1974-75)
After shave. Red with white plastic top. 5 oz. With box. **$14**

"ARMY JEEP" (1974-75)
After shave. Olive green, plastic wheels and cap. 4 oz. With box. **$18**

"BUGATTI" (1974-75)
Cologne. Black glass, chrome coloured plastic trim. 6 1/2 oz. With box. **$20**

Not illustrated:

"BIG MACK" (1973-75)
After shave. Green glass with beige flat bed and packing cases. 6 oz.
$12

"BLACK VOLKSWAGON" (1970-72)
After shave/Pre-shave. Black glass with black plastic cap. 4 oz.
$8

"CORVETTE STINGRAY '65" (1975)
After shave. Green glass, green plastic cap. 2 oz.
$12

"ELECTRIC CHARGER" (1970-72)
After shave. Black glass, red trunk and decals. With box.
$15

"MODEL A" (1972-74)
After shave. Clear glass painted yellow. 4 oz.
$8

"REO DEPOT WAGON" (1972-73)
After shave. Amber glass, black plastic top. 5 oz.
$10

"ROLLS ROYCE" (1972-75)
After shave. Clear glass painted beige, silver coloured bumper, grill and head lamps. Dark brown top and rear fenders. 6 oz.
$14

"STAGE COACH" (1970-77)
After shave. Dark amber glass with gold cargo area. 5 oz.
$10

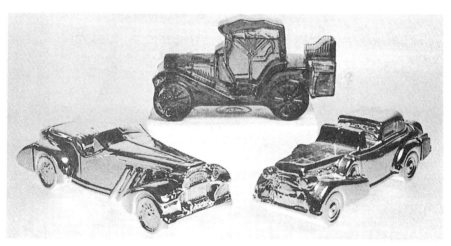

Left to Right -
"SILVER DUESENBURG" (1970-72)
After shave. Clear glass painted silver, 6 oz. **$13**

"PACKARD ROADSTER" (1970-72)
Cologne. Amber glass, amber plastic rumble seat. 6 oz. **$13**

"GOLD CADILLAC" (1969-73)
After shave. Clear glass painted gold. 6 oz. **$12**

"STOCK CAR RACER" (1974-75)
Pre-shave. Blue glass and cap. 5 oz.
With box. **$15**

"1914 STUTZ BEARCAT" (1974-77)
After shave. Painted red over clear
glass, black plastic seats and cap.
6 oz. **$8**

"55 CHEVY" (1975-76)
After shave/pre-shave. Painted green
glass with white plastic roof, fenders
and trunk. 5 oz. With box. **$16**

"STERLING 6" (1968-70)
After shave. Amber glass,
black cap. 7 oz. **$12**

"TOURING T" (1969-70)
After shave. Black glass,
black cap. 6 oz. **$12**

**"CABLE CAR DECANTER"
(1974-75)**
After shave. Painted green over
clear glass. Green and white top.
4 oz. With box **$16**

"COUNTRY VENDOR" (1973)
After shave. Brown, side decorated
with fruit and vegetables. 5 oz. **$12**

"37 CORD" (1974-76)
After shave. Glass painted yellow with plastic cap.
7 oz. **$10**

"DUNE BUGGY" (1971-73)
After shave/Hair lotion/ Bracing lotion. Blue glass, silver cap. 5 oz. **$12**

Left -
"GOLDEN ROCKET 0-2-2" (1974-76)
After shave. Smokey gold over clear glass. Copper coloured stack. 6 oz. **$14**

Right -
"CANNONBALL EXPRESS 4-6-0" (1976-77)
After shave. Black glass and cap. 3 1/4 oz. **$12**

"GENERAL 4-4-0" (1971-72)
After shave. Dark blue glass.
3 1/4 oz. **$12**

Left: **"COVERED WAGON"**
(1970-71)
After shave. Dark amber glass
wagon, with white top. 6 oz.
$10

Not illustrated:
"FERRARI '53" (1973-75)
After shave/Hair lotion.
Dark amber glass. 2 oz. **$10**

"FIRST VOLUNTEER"
(1971-72)
Cologne. Clear glass
painted gold. 6 oz. **$9**

"JAGUAR CAR DECANTER"
(1973-76)
After shave. Green glass with
green plastic trunk. 5 oz. **$12**

"MAXWELL '23 DECANTER"
(1972 -74)
After shave/Cologne. Green glass
container with beige plastic top and
trunk. 6 oz. **$14**

"STANLEY STEAMER"
(1971-72)
After shave. Blue glass with black
plastic seat and spare tire. 5 oz.
$10

"STRAIGHT 8" (1969-71)
After shave. Green glass,
black trunk. 5 oz. **$12**

"SUPER CYCLE" (1977)
Light green glass. **$9**

"THUNDERBIRD '55"
(1974-75)
After shave. Blue glass. 2 oz. **$10**

Not Illustrated
"CAPE COD 1876 COLLECTION"
(1983-84)
Candle holders. Ruby glass.
Pair **$14**

Candlestick (1975-80)
Cologne **$18**

Cruet (1975-80)
$18

Dessert Bowl and Guest Soaps
(1978-80)
$18

Salt Shakers (1978-80).
Pair **$16**

Water goblet (1976-80)
Candle holder. **$18**

Wine Decanter (1977-80)
Bubble bath. **$32**

Wine goblet (1977-80)
Fragrant candle holder. Ruby glass.
$14

Above left: **"PRESIDENT LINCOLN" (1973)**
After shave. White over clear glass, white plastic head. 6 oz. **$10**

Above right: **"PRESIDENT WASHINGTON" (1974-76)**
After shave. White over clear glass, white plastic head. 6 oz. **$10**

MUG
Marked "Avon" on base.
Opaque cream glass.
Cap with "M" above peak. **$15**

CHESS PIECE DECANTERS.
Cologne. The original set, amber glass with silver coloured caps.

Left to right :

"THE ROOK" (1973-74)	**$10**	**"SMART MOVE"** (1971-72)	**$14**
"THE KING" (1972-73)	**$14**	**"THE BISHOP"** (1974-78)	**$10**
"THE QUEEN" (1973-74)	**$14**	Not shown: **"THE PAWN"** (1974-78)	**$10**

Not shown:
CHESS PIECE DECANTERS.
Cologne. The opposing set. (1975-78) Clear glass coloured silver with plastic amber caps.

"THE ROCK II"	**$9**	**"SMART MOVE II"**	**$9**
"THE KING II"	**$9**	**"THE BISHOP II"**	**$9**
"THE QUEEN II"	**$9**	**"THE PAWN II"**	**$9**

"BEER MUG DECANTER"
After shave. Clear glass with white top. 4 oz. With box. **$14**

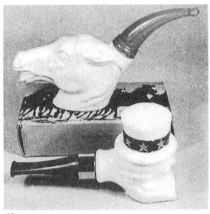

Above:
"WILD MUSTANG PIPE DECANTER" (1976-77)
Cologne. Painted white over clear glass. 3 oz. With box. **$10**

"UNCLE SAM PIPE" (1975-76)
After shave. Opaque white glass, blue hat band and plastic stem. 3 oz. **$8**

"COLLECTOR'S PIPE DECANTER"(1973-74)
After shave. Brown glass, black stem, gold band. 3 oz. **$12**

Above left:
"DUTCH PIPE" (1973-74)
Cologne. Opaque white glass with blue decoration, silver coloured stem and cap. 2 oz. **$10**

Above right -
"PONY EXPRESS RIDER PIPE DECANTER" (1975-76)
Cologne. Opaque white glass with black plastic stem. 3 oz. **$9**

Above :
"BULL DOG PIPE DECANTER" (1972-73)
After shave/Cologne. Opaque white glass with black stem. 6 oz. **$10**

Left :
"PIPE FULL" (1971-72)
After shave. Brown glass, black stem. 2 oz. **$8**

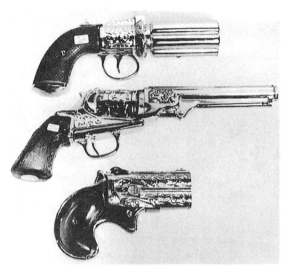

Top to bottom:

"1850 PEPPERBOX" (1976-77)
After shave. Silver over glass barrel, gold and brown plastic handle. 3 oz. **$9**

"1851 COLT REVOLVER" (1975-76)
After shave. Amber glass handle with silver plastic trigger, barrel and chamber. 3 oz. **$12**

"DERRINGER" (1977)
Amber glass handle with gold coloured barrel. 2 oz. **$18**

Right to left:

"1780 BLUNDERBUSS PISTOL" (1976)
After shave. Dark amber glass, gold plastic cap and trigger. 5 1/2 oz. **$15**

"1760 DUELLING PISTOL" (1973-74)
After shave. Brown glass, silvered cap and trigger. 4 oz. **$15**

"DUELLING PISTOL II" (1975)
After shave. Black glass, gold plastic cap and trigger. 4 oz. **$13**

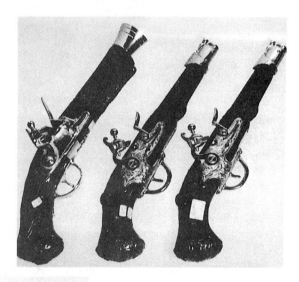

"1850 PEPPERBOX PISTOL" (1976-77)
After shave. Silver over glass barrel, gold and brown plastic handle. 3 oz. With box. **$14**

Left to right -

"COLEMAN LANTERN" (1977-79)

After shave. Painted green over clear glass, green cap. 5 oz. **$12**

"CAPITOL DECANTER" (1970-72)

After shave. Amber glass with gold cap. 5 oz. **$7**

"FIRST CLASS MALE" (1970-71)

Hair lotion. Blue glass, red cap. 4 oz. **$7**

Left to right :

"KING PIN" (1969-70)

After shave. Opaque white glass, red label and stripes. 4 oz. **$7**

"SNOOPY SURPRISE" (1969-71)

After shave. Opaque white glass, blue or yellow cap, black ears. 5 oz. **$8**

"REMEMBER WHEN GAS PUMP" (1976-77)

After shave. Painted red over clear glass. Red and white plastic cap. 4 oz. **$12**

Left to right:

"WILD WEST BULLET" (1977-78)

After shave. Bronze over clear glass, silver top. 1 1/2 oz. **$5**

"BARBER SHOP BRUSH" (1976)

Cologne. Brown glass, brown and white top. 1 1/2 oz. **$10**

"BARBER POLE" (1974-75)

After shave/Conditioner. Opaque white glass, red and blue paper label, white plastic cap. 3 oz. **$9**

"CHAMPION SPARK PLUG"

After shave. Opaque white glass, gray cap. 1 1/2 oz. **$4**

AVON CERAMIC STEINS.

Each stein originally sold with an 8 ounce container of men's cologne.

Left to Right:

"CAR CLASSIC" (1979)   **$60**

"SPORTING STEIN" (1978)   **$60**

"WESTERN ROUND-UP" (1980)   **$60**

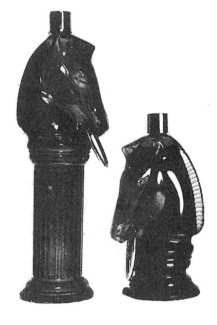

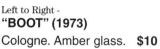

Left to Right -

"BOOT" (1973)
Cologne. Amber glass.   **$10**

"WEATHER-OR-NOT" (1969-71)
After shave. Dark amber glass.
5 oz.   **$8**

"PONY POST IMPERATOR" (1972)
Green glass with gold cap
and ring.   **$12**

"SHORT PONY DECANTER" (1968-69)
Pre-shave. Green glass, gold cap
and ring. 4 oz.   **$8**

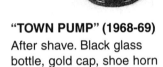

"IRON HORSE SHAVING MUG" (1974-76)

After shave. Opaque white glass mug, plastic bottle, gold cap. 7 oz. With box. **$12**

"TOWN PUMP" (1968-69)

After shave. Black glass bottle, gold cap, shoe horn handle. 6 oz. **$12**

Below:
"TOTEM POLE DECANTER" (1975)

After shave. Amber glass and cap. 6 oz. **$10**

Above:
"TOTEM POLE DECANTER" (1975)

After shave. Amber glass and cap. 6 oz. **$10**

Left to right:
"STRAWBERRY BATH FOAM" (1971-72)

Red glass. 4 oz. **$9**

"AVON BEAUTY DUST SHAKER"

Coloured cranberry over clear glass, silver top. **$8**

"WHALE OIL LANTERN DECANTER" (1974-75)

After shave. Green glass, silver plastic top and base. 5 oz. **$12**

"ZODIAC HOROSCOPE" (1977)

After shave. Amber glass with gold and black label. Came in 12 zodiac signs. 4 oz. **$10**

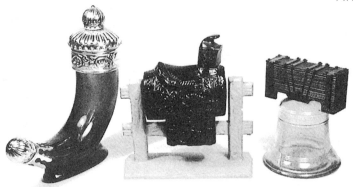

Left to right -
"VIKING HORN" (1966)

After shave. Amber glass with gold decoration. 7 oz. **$16**

"WESTERN SADDLE" (1971-72)

After shave. Brown glass and cap, beige fence. 5 oz. **$10**

"LIBERTY BELL" (1971-72)

After shave/Cologne. Amber glass, brown cap. 4 oz. **$7**

Not shown -
"HIGHWAY KING" (1977-79)

Transport with green glass cab containing after shave (4 oz.). White plastic trailer and wheels, rear section of trailer is white plastic bottle containing talc. **$15**

"PHEASANT DECANTER" (1972-74)

After shave. Brown glass with green pheasant head cap. 5 oz. **$10**

Left to right -
"HOMESTEAD DECANTER" (1973-74)

Pre-shave. Brown glass, gray plastic chimney. 4 oz. **$6**

"PONY EXPRESS" (1971-72)

After shave. Brown glass, copper coloured rider. 5 oz. **$14**

"SIDE WHEELER" (1971-72)

After shave. Amber glass with plastic smoke stacks, silver cap. 5 oz. **$8**

"KODIAK BEAR" (1977)
After shave. Dark amber glass bottle with plastic cap. 6 oz. With box. **$22**

"ELECTRIC GUITAR DECANTER" (1974-75)
After shave. Brown glass, silver plastic cap. 6 oz. With box. **$15**

Left to right:
"TALL SHIPS MINIATURE STEIN" (1982-83)
Ceramic, numbered and dated on base. Ht. 4 1/2". **$15**

"TABATHA COLOGNE SPRAY" (1975-76)
Black glass and cap. 3 oz. **$8**

"TRIBUTE SILVER WARRIOR" (1967)
After shave. Plastic silver helmet over blue glass bottle. 6 oz. **$8**

Left to right:
"PONY POST" (1972-73)
After shave. Bronze over clear glass, bronze cap. 5 oz. **$12**

"GRACEFUL GIRAFFE" (1976)
Cologne. Clear glass, gold plastic cap. 1 1/2 oz. **$6**

"AVON CALLING FOR MEN"
Cologne. Painted gold over clear glass. Black plastic cap and receiver. 6 oz. **$14**

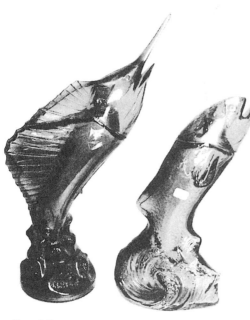

"CANADA GOOSE DECANTER" (1973-74)
After shave/Cologne. Brown glass, black plastic cap. 5 oz. **$10**

Above left:
"SEA TROPHY" (1972)
After shave. Blue glass with blue plastic fish head cap. 5 1/2 oz. **$10**

Above right:
"RAINBOW TROUT DECANTER" (1973-74)
After shave. Green glass with green plastic cap. 5 oz. **$9**

"MALLARD DUCK" (1967-68)
After shave. Green glass with silver coloured head. 6 oz. **$12**

Left to right:
"WINE SERVER" (1972) Cologne. Green glass. **$18**

"PAID STAMP" (1970-71) After shave. Dark amber glass with black cap. 4 oz. **$8**

"POT BELLY STOVE" (1970-71) After shave. Black glass. 5 oz. **$7**

Left to right:

"NOBLE PRINCE" (1975-77)
After shave/pre-shave. Brown glass
and cap. 4 oz. **$8**

"FAITHFUL LADDIE" (1977-79)
After shave. Amber glass.
4 oz. **$8**

"GENTLE FOAL" (1979-80)
Cologne. Amber glass and cap.
1 1/2 oz. **$6**

Above left:
"MAJESTIC ELEPHANT" (1977)
After shave. Clear glass painted
gray. 5 1/2 oz. With box. **$20**

Above right:
**"THE AMERICAN BUFFALO"
(1975-76)**
After shave. Amber glass, plastic
buffalo head cap with ivory
horns. 5 oz. With box. **$15**

Below left:
"ALASKAN MOOSE" (1974-75)
After shave. Amber glass with
cream coloured plastic antlers.
8 oz. With box. **$26**

Left to right:

"VANITY JAR" (1975-76)
Rich Moisture Cream. Clear glass, silvered top, 5 oz. **$5**

"PERFUMED PEDESTAL CANDLE CONTAINER" Clear glass, painted amber (1965-1966) Ht. 6 1/4". **$12**
Also comes in clear painted red. **$16**

"FOSTORIA EGG SOAP DISH" (1977 second issue)
Clear glass with "Spring Lilac" scented soap. **$19**
First issue marked "Mother's Day 1977". **$23**

Above:

"BUTTER DISH" (1973-74)
Clear glass. Sold originally with three yellow hostess soaps. **$12.50**

Below left to right:

"SKIN-SO-SOFT DECANTER" (1967)
Bath Oil. Clear glass, cork stopper with glass finial, 8oz. **$6.50**

"SEA HORSE" (1970-72)
Bath Oil. Clear glass, gold cap, 6 oz. **$8**

Left to right. All complete and with boxes:

"STRAWBERRY PORCELAIN PLATE" (1978) $30

"STRAWBERRY PORCELAIN DEMI CUP CANDLETTE" (1979-80) $21

"STRAWBERRY PORCELAIN NAPKIN RING" (1978) $15

Above left to right:

"WINTER FROLICS HOSTESS SOAPS" (1977-78)

With box. **$12**

"CORAL EMPRESS POMANDER" (1975)

Coral colour wax figure. Ht. 6 1/2" **$9**

"REVOLUTIONARY SOLDIER SMOKER'S CANDLE" (1979-80)

Clear or amber glass. Clear harder to find. With box. **$15**

"HEART & DIAMOND FOSTORIA LOVING CUP PERFUMED CANDLE HOLDER" (1978)

Clear glass. On base "Avon '78 Exclusive Avon Design" **$20**

"ANNIVERSARY KEEPSAKE"

Cologne, note old style California Perfume Co. design and label.

Left :
1979. Clear glass, silver cap.
3/4 oz. With box. **$9**

Right:
1978-79. Clear glass, pink ribbon.
1 1/2 oz. With box. **$9**

Above left to right:
"ROSES CREAM SACHET"
(1972-75) Pink or clear glass jar.
2/3 oz. With box. **$6**

"HAWAIIAN WHITE GINGER COLOGNE MIST" (1972-76)

Clear glass bottle, green, red and white cap under clear plastic. 2 oz. With box. **$8**

"HAWAIIAN WHITE GINGER CREAM SACHET" (1973-78)

Clear glass jar with green red and white lid. 2/3 oz. With box. **$2**

Above left to right:
"LA BELLE TELEPHONE"
(1974-76) Perfume. Clear glass, gold top. 1 oz. With box. **$11**

"HEARTH LAMP" (1973-76)

Bubble bath. Black glass with yellow and white plastic shade. 8 oz. With box. **$14**

Left -
"CRYSTAL POINT SALT SHAKERS" (1976-77)

Cologne. Blue glass, lucite tops. 1 1/2 oz. Pair with boxes. **$15**

"DUTCH GIRL FIGURINE COLOGNE" (1973-74)

Blue painted glass, light blue plastic top. 3 oz. With box. **$12**

"SKATER'S WALTZ DECANTERS" (1977-78)

Cologne. Red flock over clear glass, pink plastic top. Also comes in blue. 4 oz. **$15**

Left to Right:

"TO A WILD ROSE TOILET WATER" (1956-62)

Opaque white glass, pink stopper. 2 oz. **$9**

"IMPERIAL GARDEN COLOGNE MIST" (1973-77)

White glass decorated with orange flowers. 3 oz. **$5**

"BLUE DEMI-CUP" (1968-70)

Cologne. Opaque white glass, blue scene and cap. 3 oz. **$8**

Left:

"AVONSHIRE BLUE SOAP DISH" (1972)

Oval, trimmed with white. **$8**

Right:

"AVONSHIRE BLUE BATH OIL DECANTER" (1979)

With white trim. 6 oz. **$12**

Left to right:

"LITTLE GIRL BLUE" (1972-73)

Cologne. Painted blue over clear glass with blue plastic top. 3 oz. **$7**

"GARDEN GIRL" (1975)

Cologne. Yellow top with frosted glass base. 4 oz. **$7**

"FLOWER MAIDEN" (1973-74)

Cologne. Painted yellow over clear glass, white plastic top. **$9**

Not shown -

"LITTLE DREAM GIRL" (1980-81)

Cologne. Pale lustred blue over clear glass, cream coloured top. 1 1/4 oz. **$7**

Left:

"ANGEL SONG" (1978-79)

Cologne. Frosted glass base, off white top. 1 oz. **$6**

Right:

"ANGEL SONG WITH MANDOLIN" (1979-80)

Cologne. Frosted glass base, white top. 1 oz. **$6**

Left:

"AMERICAN BELL" (1976-78)

Cologne. Painted yellow over clear glass, yellow cap. 4 oz. **$7**

Right:

"DUTCH MAID" (1977-79)

Cologne. Painted blue over clear glass, blue plastic top. 4 oz. **$10**

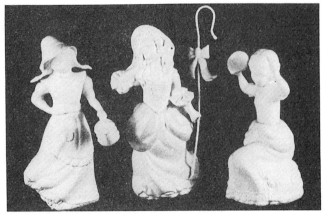

Left to right:
"MARY MARY"
(1977-79)
Cologne. Frosted white over opaque glass, white top. 2 oz. **$9**

"LITTLE BO-PEEP"
(1979-80)
Cologne. Painted white over opaque glass, white plastic top and shepherd's staff. 2 oz. **$12**

"LITTLE MISS MUFFET" (1978-80)
Cologne. White over opaque glass, white plastic top. 2 oz. **$10**

Left to right:
"BETSY ROSS" (1976)
Cologne. Painted white over clear glass. 4 oz. **$10**

"GOOD FAIRY" (1978-80)
Cologne. Painted blue over clear glass. Blue plastic top, pink and blue fabric wings and purse. 3 oz. **$12**

"18TH CENTURY CLASSIC FIGURINE YOUNG GIRL" (1974-75)
Bath oil. White over clear glass, white plastic head. 4 oz. **$9**

"VICTORIAN LADY" (1972-73)
Bath oil. Opaque white glass, plastic cap. 5 oz. **$10**

Left to right:

"FRAGRANCE TOUCH" (1969-70)
Cologne. Opaque white glass.
3 oz. **$10**

"SOMEWHERE POWDER SACHET" (1966-68)
Opaque white glass, gold band
on lid. 9/10 oz.
No label. **$6**   With label **$18**

"GRECIAN PITCHER" (1972-76)
Bath oil. Opaque white glass.
5 oz. **$11**

"ROYAL SWAN COLOGNE" (1971-72)
Opaque white glass, gold crown.
1 oz. **$8**

"PERFUMED PEDESTAL CANDLE CONTAINER" (1964-66)
Opaque white glass. **$20**

Left:
"BRIDAL MOMENTS" (1976-79)
Cologne. Clear glass painted white.
White plastic cap. 5 oz.
$18

Right:
"PROUD GROOM" (1979-80)
Cologne. Clear glass
painted white. 2 oz.
$20

Left to Right:

"SITTING PRETTY" (1976-77)
Cologne. Opaque white glass
base with pink bows, plastic top.
1 1/2 oz. **$8**

"KITTEN LITTLE" (1972-76)
Cologne. Painted white over
clear glass. 1 1/2 oz. **$7**

"CHURCH MOUSE BRIDE" (1978-79)
Cologne. Matt finish over opaque
white glass. White plastic top
with veil. 2 oz. **$10**

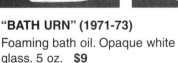

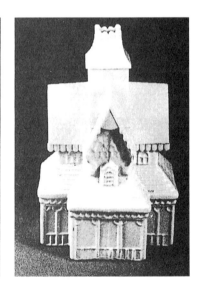

"BATH URN" (1971-73)
Foaming bath oil. Opaque white
glass. 5 oz. **$9**

"MING CAT COLOGNE" (1971)
Opaque glass with blue decoration
and ribbon. 6 oz. **$10**

**"VICTORIAN MANOR
COLOGNE DECANTER"
(1972-73)**
Clear glass painted pink
with pink plastic roof. 5 oz.
$12

Left to Right -
"HOBNAIL BUD VASE" (1973-74)
Cologne. Opaque white glass decorated with pink and yellow roses. 4 oz. **$12**
"ROYAL COACH" (1972-73)
Bath oil. Opaque white glass, gold cap. 5 oz. **$8**
"CORNUCOPIA" (1971-76)
Bath oil. Opaque white glass, gold cap. 6 oz. **$7**

"STRAWBERRIES & CREAM BATH OIL" (1970)
Opaque white glass with red top. 4 oz. **$10**

Left to Right:
"LEISURE HOURS" (1970-72)
Bath oil. Opaque white glass.
5 oz. **$10**

"FRAGRANCE HOURS COLOGNE" (1971-73)
Opaque ivory glass. 6 oz. **$10**

"ARMOIRE DECANTER" (1972-75)
Bath oil. Opaque white glass.
5 oz. **$9**

Above left to right:

"COURTING LAMP" (1970-71)
Cologne. Blue glass font with opaque white glass shade. 5 oz. **$10**

"MANSION LAMP" (1975-76)
Cologne. Blue glass, white plastic cap. 6 oz. **$15**

"PARLOUR LAMP" (1971-72)
Frosted yellow glass font contained talcum powder, gold coloured cap over top section contained cologne. **$10**

"TIFFANY LAMP" (1972-74)
Cologne. Brown glass with flowers on pink shade. 5 oz. **$15**

"CHIMNEY LAMP COLOGNE MIST DECANTER" (1973-74)
Cologne. 2 oz. Clear or patterned glass base with plastic chimney. Each **$8**

"MING BLUE LAMP" (1974-76)
Bath oil. Blue glass with white plastic shade. 5 oz. **$8**

"COUNTRY JUG" (1976-78)
Hand lotion. Painted gray over clear glass, blue decoration. 10 oz. **$8**

"ISLAND PARAKEET" (1977-78)

Cologne. Blue glass, blue and yellow plastic top. 1 1/2 oz. With box. **$8**

"AVON CALLING 1905" (1973)

After shave. Brown glass with gold bell, black receiver. 7 oz. With box. **$15**

"VICTORIAN SEWING BASKET" (1974-76)

Moisture cream. Opaque white glass with lavender plastic top. 5 oz. With box. **$12**

"PETIT-POINT CREAM SACHET" (1974-76)

Amethyst jar with gold lid. 1 oz. With box. **$10**

"SEWING NOTIONS" (1975)

Cologne. Pink and white glass with silver cap. 1 oz. With box. **$8**

"ORIENTAL EGG CHINESE PHEASANT" (1975)

Cologne. White decorated opal glass egg on black plastic base. 1 oz. With box. **$12**

Above left to right:

"HOSPITALITY BELL" (1976-77)
Cologne. Blue glass bell, silver
handle. 3 3/4 oz. With box.   **$12**

"ROSE POINT BELL" (1978)
Cologne. Red and clear glass bell
with clear handle. 4 oz.   **$15**

"CRYSTAL SONG BELL" (1975-76)
Cologne. Ruby glass bell with frosted
handle and bow. 4 oz.   **$15**

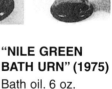

Left to right:

**"MOONLIGHT GLOW
ANNUAL BELL"**
(1981-82)
Cologne. Green glass
bell, frosted handle.
3 oz. **$15**

"HOBNAIL BELL"
(1973-79)
Cologne. Opaque
white glass,
gold handle. 2 oz. **$8**

"EMERALD BELL"
(1978-79)
Cologne. Light green
glass bell, gold and
green plastic handle.
3 3/4 oz. **$12**

**"APOTHECARY
DECANTER"** (1973-76)
Came in light green,
blue/green and light
yellow glass. 8 oz. **$10**

**"NILE GREEN
BATH URN"** (1975)
Bath oil. 6 oz.
$10

Left to right:

"PEAR LUMIERE" (1975-76)

Cologne mist. Clear glass with clear plastic cap. 2 oz. **$8**

"SONG OF SPRING" (1977)

Cologne. Frosted glass with frosted plastic cap and blue plastic bird. 1 oz. **$8**

"SONG BIRD COLOGNE" (1971)

Clear glass. 1 1/2 oz. **$9**

"KEEPSAKE CREAM SACHET" (1970-73)

Frosted glass with metal lid. 3/4 oz. **$9**

"FRAGRANCE BELL COLOGNE" (1968-69)

Clear glass, gold coloured cap. 1 oz. **$10**

Not shown:

"COLOGNE GELEE" (1971-72)

Green jar, orange plastic lid. 3 oz. **$3**

"EMERALD BUD VASE" (1971-72)

Cologne. Green glass. 3 oz. **$9**

Left to right -

"TREE MOUSE" (1977-79)

Cream sachet. Clear glass with clear plastic top, gold mouse. 2/3 oz. **$5**

"SNOWMAN" (1975)

Cream sachet. Opaque white glass, pink hat. 1 oz. **$5**

"JOYOUS BELL" (1978)

Cologne. Frosted light blue over clear glass, silver top. **$4**

"SNOW BIRD" (1973-74)

Cream sachet. Opaque white glass, plastic top. 1 1/2 oz. **$5**

Left to right:

"FLUTTERING FANCY DECANTER" (1980)

Cologne. Clear glass, yellow lid with pink butterfly. 1 oz. **$7**

"JOLLY SANTA" (1978-79)

Cologne. Clear glass, white beard, red cap. 1 oz. **$4**

"CHRISTMAS SURPRISE" (1976)

Cologne. Green glass, with red or silver cap. 1 oz. **$3.50**

"BON BON COLOGNE" (1972-73)

Opaque white poodle with white cap. 1 oz. **$6**

"DAPPER SNOWMAN" (1978-79)

Cologne. Opaque white glass with black features and hat. 1 oz. **$5**

"TEDDY BEAR COLOGNE" (1976-78)

Frosted glass with gold cap. 3/4 oz. **$5**

Left - Right -

"ROBIN RED BREAST COLOGNE DECANTER" (1974-75)

Silver plastic over frosted red glass. 2 oz. **$5**

"GOOD LUCK ELEPHANT" (1978)

Cologne. Silver plastic head, frosted glass. 43 ml. **$12**

"OWL FANCY COLOGNE GELEE" (1974-76)

Gold plastic head on clear glass. 4 oz. **$6**

Representative Awards

Above:
**FOUR SEASONS
AWARD DOLLS (1980)**
Awarded to Canadian Sales
Representatives. Ceramic figures
marked "Rex, Valencia, Spain."
Left to right:
Spring, Summer, Autumn, Winter.
The set **$125**

*The Wild Flowers Award Plates
were made in England by Enoch
Wedgwood (Tunstall) Ltd.,
exclusively for Avon Products Inc.*

Above:
**WILD FLOWERS
AWARD PLATE (1976-78)**
"Wild Flowers of the Northern
United States". Mallow, Buttercup,
Pipsissewa and Purple Cornflower
on white ground. **$60**

Right:
**WILD FLOWERS
AWARD PLATE (1976-78)**
"Wild Flowers of the Western
United States".Columbine, Bed
Straw, Pickle Poppy and California
Poppy on white ground. **$60**

Christmas Plates

AVON CHRISTMAS PLATES

1974
"Country Church"   **$65**

1975
"Christmas on the Farm"   **$55**

1976
"Bringing Home the Tree"   **$50**

1979
"Dashing Through the Snow"   **$40**

1981
"Sharing the Christmas Spirit"   **$35**

Beers

Beer is often referred to as the universal drink and is probably the oldest alcoholic beverage made by man. Beer has been brewed in Canada since the first settlers arrived. Prior to being sold in bottles, barrels or kegs were the containers used for beer. It was during the 1790's that quart bottles came into use and by 1839 pint size bottles were available. Many beer bottles were embossed with the brewer's name. Paper labels were first used on Canadian beers in 1875. Examples of early embossed or labeled bottles are scarce but it is possible to assemble a collection dating from the early 1900's.

Before the introduction of the amber "stubby" bottle in 1962 Canadian breweries packaged their product in long neck bottles of various shapes and colours; amber, clear and green. The "Stubby" was introduced first in the provinces of Ontario, Quebec, Newfoundland, Prince Edward Island, Nova Scotia and New Brunswick. Breweries in British Columbia and Manitoba began using this type of bottle in 1963, and the Saskatchewan and Alberta breweries followed in 1964. The "stubby" or "compact" bottle was convenient for the brewers as it was uniform throughout Canada. However in the early 1980's the shape of beer bottles began to change again, the "stubby" bottle was being phased out and breweries were again packaging their product in various shapes and colours of long neck bottles.

In 1861 there were 182 active breweries in Canada, however, over the years, prohibition, wars, recessions and business consolidations have caused a decrease in the number of Canadian companies. In 1989 the two major brewing companies in Canada, Molson-Carling (merger of 1989) and Labatt's serve 96% of the domestic market from their plants across the country.

Much information can be found from the embossing or labels on bottles and many collectors find themselves becoming interested in the history of the breweries and search business directories and other publications in libraries for facts pertaining to the many changes in the Canadian brewing industry.

BEER. A fermented malt beverage. Varying amounts of the basic ingredients, malt, hops, water, sometimes with the addition of rice or corn are used in each brew. The method of brewing, using either a top-fermenting or a bottom-fermenting yeast, accounts for the taste difference between the types of beer.

ALE – is brewed using a top-fermenting yeast. More hops than used in a lager brew are added to the ingredients giving ale a stronger taste than lager.

BOCK – a dark heavy and rather sweet lager brewed during the winter for the spring market.

LAGER – made using less hops than in ale. Lager is brewed using a bottom-fermenting yeast and is a lighter tasting beer than ale.

PORTER/STOUT – top-fermented. Additional ingredients, such as roasted malt or barley, malted or flaked oats or barley and various sugars are added to the ingredients used in ale making.

BOTTLES
• Large, 22 ounces, referred to as a quart.
• Small, 12 ounces, referred to as a pint.
• Split, 6 to 8 ounces.

CANS. The sale of Canadian beer in cans during the early 1960's was less than one percent of packaged beer sales. By the late 1980's the sale of Canadian beer in cans had risen to 16.3%.

MATCHING CAP. Type of cap originally used by brewery.

BREWERIES. In 1861 there were 182 active breweries in Canada today there are 63 brewing plants across the country, 26 of these are microbreweries.

MICROBREWERY. Produces less than one million cases of beer each year.

PROHIBITION. Prohibited the manufacture and importation of alcoholic beverages containing more than 2 1/2% of proof spirits. In some jurisdictions, there were exceptions, in Ontario, for example legislation prohibited the sale of alcoholic liquors, except native wine, for purposes other than medicinal or scientific. In Quebec the sale of light beer (not more than 2.5% alcohol by volume weight) and light wine and cider (not more than 6.94% alcohol by volume weight) was permitted. Commencing in 1916 one province after another introduced prohibition legislation and in 1918 the Federal Government prohibited the manufacture and importation of liquors containing more than 2 1/2% of proof spirits. During the 1920's and 30's each jurisdiction, one by one, repealed prohibition legislation.

Left:
**"BERLIN LION BREWERY,
C.N. Huether Prop.,
Berlin, Ont."**
Amber, Ht. 10"
Early 1900's **$80**

Centre:
"BERLIN LION BREWERY"
Pilsener Beer.
Clear pint. BIMAL.
Ca. 1910. Chipped. **$20**

Right:
"NEW PREMIUM ALE"
Blue Top Brewing Co. Ltd.
Kitchener, Ont. Green pint
with contents.
Late 1940's. **$12**

Left to right :
"OLDE TYME STOCK ALE"
Huether's Brewing Co. Ltd.,
Kitchener, Ont. Green pint.
Late 1900's. **$12**

"BLUE TOP BEER"
Blue Top Brewing Co. Ltd.,
Kitchener, Ont. Clear pint.
Late 1930's - early 1940's. **$15**

"BLUE TOP ALE"
Blue Top Brewing Co. Green pint.
Mid 1940's. **$15**

"RANGER LAGER"
Ranger Brewing Co. Ltd.,
Kitchener, Ont. Clear pint.
1952-56. **$15**

"RANGER ALE"
Ranger Brewing Co. Ltd.
Green pint, 1952-56. **$15**

BAVARIAN BREWING LTD.,
St. John's, Newfoundland.
Left to right:
"RED LABEL OLD STOCK BEER"
Clear pint with contents. Late 1950's. **$12**

"JOCKEY CLUB BEER"
Clear pint. Late 1950's. **$7**

"BLUE STAR"
Clear pint with contents. Late 1950's. **$12**

"SILVER SPRING ALE"
Silver Spring Brewery,
Sherbrooke, Quebec.
Green pint. Late 1930's,
early 1940's. **$15**

Left:
"ROCK SPRINGS LAGER BEER"
Rock Brewery Ltd., Preston, Ont.
Amber pint. 1929. **$40**

Centre:
"ROB ROY ALE"
Walkerville Brewery Ltd.,
Walkerville, Ontario.
Green pint. 1940's. **$15**

Right:
**"OLD STYLE EXPORT
LAGER BEER"**
Walkerville Brewery Ltd.
Clear pint. Late 1940's **$20**

BLACKWOOD BROS.,
Winnipeg, Manitoba.
Left -
"BLACKWOODS"
On reverse "Winnipeg"
On base "B". Aqua, BIMAL.
1890's. **$30**

Right :
"BLACKWOODS, Winnipeg"
"Anyone filling, buying, selling or
destroying this bottle will be
prosecuted"
On base "Our Trademark" with "BB"
in a triangle. 1890's. **$30**

THE DREWRY'S LIMITED,
Winnipeg, Manitoba.

Left to right:
"OLD STOCK ALE"
Clear pint. Late 1940's. **$10**

"OLD CABIN ALE"
Amber pint with matching cap.
Late 1930's, early 1940's. **$15**

"OLD STOCK ALE"
Green pint. Late 1930's
early 1940's. **$10**

"STANDARD LAGER"
Amber pint. 1950's. **$10**

Left to right:

"PAT'S GOLD BAND RICE BEER"
Lake-of-the-Woods Brewing Co., Kenora, Ontario.
Clear pint. 1940's. **$12**

"BECK'S PILSENER"
Beck Brewing Co. Ltd., Ford Frances, Ont.
Clear pint. Late 1950's early 1960's. **$7**

"WHITE LABEL ALE"
Cosgrave-Dominion Brewery Ltd., Toronto, Ontario.
Green pint. Late 1930's. **$12**

"OLD STOCK ALE"
Perth Brewery, Stratford, Ontario.
Green pint. 1930's. **$12**

Left:
"JOHN GOMPF ONTARIO BREWERY" (Hamilton)
Slightly suncast. Ht. 10".
Early 1900's. **$40**

Centre:
"ROBT. DAVIES DOMINION BREWERY, Toronto"
Aqua, BIMAl. Ht. 9 1/4."
1890's. **$100**

Right:
"AULD STYLE SCOTCH ALE"
Cosgrave Export Brewing Co., Toronto, Ont.
Green pint. 1940's. **$15**

Left:
"BUDWEISER ALE"
Brewing Corp. of Canada
Ltd., Waterloo, Ontario.
Green pint. 1940's. **$6**

Centre:
"CANADA BUD BEER"
Canada Bud Breweries
Limited, Toronto, Ont.
Clear pint. Late 1940's,
early 1950's. **$8**

Right :
"CANADA BUD ALE"
Canada Bud Breweries
Limited.
Green pint. 1950's. **$10**

Left to right:
"REGAL"
Regal Brewing Co.,
Hamilton, Ontario.
Green quart.
Late 1920's - 30's. **$15**

"EXPORT LAGER"
Strathroy Brewing &
Malting Co.,

Strathroy, Ontario.
Clear pint. 1930's. **$10**

"AMBER ALE"
Reinhardt Brewing Co.,
Toronto, Ontario.
Green pint. Early
1930's. **$12**

"EXTRA STOCK ALE"
Taylor & Bates Ltd.,
Hamilton, Ontario.
Amber quart.
1936-37. **$15**

NATIONAL BREWERIES LTD., Quebec, Quebec.

Left to right:

"BOSWELL CREAM PORTER"
Green quart. Late 1920's – early 1930's. **$12**

"BOSWELL'S EXPORT ALE"
Green pint with matching cap.
Early to mid 1930's. **$15**

"BOSWELL GREEN LABEL ALE"
Green quart with matching cap. 1940's **$12**

"BOSWELL CREAM PORTER"
Green quart. 1940's. **$12**

**"BOSWELL
GREEN LABEL ALE"**
National Breweries Ltd.
Green pint. Non-
returnable. 1940's. **$7**

WM. DOW & COMPANY.
Montreal, Quebec.
Left to Right -
"INDIA PALE ALE"
Green quart. Pre-1900. **$40**

"PALE ALE"
Green pint. Ca. 1915. **$20**

"CROWN STOUT"
Green pint with matching cap.
Late 1930's – early 1940's.
$12

"PALE BITTER ALE"
Green quart with matching
cap. Late 1930's.
On neck label "By appoint-
ment to His Excellency Lord
Tweedsmuir, Governor
General of Canada." **$15**

Left to right:

"DOW ALE" Green pint. Late 1950's.   **$4**

"DOW ALE" Green pint. Non-returnable. Late 1940's.   **$4**

"DOW ALE"Green pint. Non-returnable. Late 1940's.   **$3**

"CHAMPLAIN CREAM PORTER" Dow Brewery Limited, Montreal, Quebec. Green pint. Late 1950's.   **$5**

DOW BREWERY LIMITED.

Left to right:

"DOW ALE"
Green, quart.
Mid 1940's.   **$6**

"KINGSBEER" Clear quart. Late 1950's.   **$5**

"CHAMPLAIN CREAM PORTER"
Green quart. Late 1950's.   **$8**

"DOW ALE" Green quart. Late 1950's.   **$6**

"DOW ALE" Left:
Green pint with contents.
Non-returnable. 1940's.   **$10**
Right:
Experimental stubby.
Label on back "25th April 1961".
Amber pint with contents.   **$10**

DOW BREWERIES LIMITED.
Mid 1960's.
"KEBEC" Green quart.   **$7**
"KEBEC" Green stubby pint.   **$7**

"EKERS EXPORT LAGER"
(Montreal).
Dark amber pint. BIMAL.
Hand finished neck –
Pre-1910.   **$40**

FRONTENAC BREWERIES LIMITED,
Montreal, Quebec. Left to right:
"WHITE CAP ALE"
Green pint. Non-returnable. 1940's.   **$8**
"BLUE LABEL"
Clear pint. Non-returnable. 1940's.   **$8**
"SPECIAL LAGER BEER"
Green pint. Late 1950's.   **$7**

BRADING'S.
Left to right -
"STAG'S HEAD LAGER BEER"
Clear quart with contents.
1950's. **$20**

"CRYSTAL ALE"
Green quart, empty.
1950's. **$15**

"OLD STOCK ALE"
Green pint. 1950's. **$6**

BRADING'S. Left to right:
"PORTER" Green pint with matching cap.
Mid 1950's. **$8**

"CINCINNATI CREAM LAGER"
Clear pint. Mid 1950's. **$8**

"ALE" Green pint with matching cap.
Mid 1950's. **$8**

"CINCINNATI CREAM LAGER"
British American
Brewing Co.,
Windsor, Ontario.
Clear pint. Late 1940's.
$10

BRADING DISPLAY STAND.
Mid 1960's. From a Quebec store.
Gilded metal. Ht. 8 1/2" Length 10".
With bottles and can. **$25**

CAPITAL BREWING CO. LIMITED, Ottawa, Ontario. Left to right:

"EXPORT LAGER"
Clear quart. Ca. 1910. **$15**

"SELECT STOCK CAPITAL ALE"
Green quart. 1930's. **$15**

"OLD STOCK CAPITAL ALE"
Green quart. 1930's. **$15**

"OLD STOCK CAPITAL ALE"
Green quart. 1930's. **$15**

"OLD STOCK CAPITAL ALE"
Green quart. Mid 1940's. **$15**

Not shown:
"OLD STOCK CAPITAL ALE"
Green quart. 1950's. **$15**

THE BRADING BREWING CO., Ottawa, Ontario.
"PALE ALE" bottles from the early 1900's. All 12 oz. (pint).
Three on left – amber, bottle at right green.   **Each $50**

Left to right:

"BRADING'S OLD STOCK ALE"
Green quart. Late 1930's.   **$8**

"BRADING'S BROWN STOUT"
Green pint. Late 1930's.   **$15**

"BRADING'S JUBILEE PORTER"
Green pint. Late 1950's.   **$8**

"JUBILEE ALE" Jubilee Brewery
Limited, Toronto, Ontario.
Green pint. 1950's.   **$8**

CALGARY BREWING & MALTING COMPANY LIMITED, Calgary, Alberta.

Left to right:

"PALE ALE"
Amber pint. 1950's.   **$8 - $12**

"BEER"
Amber pint. 1950's.   **$8 - $12**

"STOCK ALE"
Amber pint. 1950's   **$8 - $12**

"STOUT XXXX"
Amber pint. 1950's.   **$8 - $12**

"STAMPEDE PILSENER"
Amber pint. 1950's.   **$8 - $12**

"PILSENER"
Amber pint. 1960's.   **$8 - $12**

Left:
"CALGARY BREWING & MALTING COMPANY LTD."
Clear pint. BIMAL.
Late 1800's.   **$50**

Centre:
"STAMPEDE BEER"
Calgary Brewing & Malting
Company Ltd.,
Amber pint. 1950's.   **$10**

Right:
"CHINOOK BEER"
Calgary Brewing & Malting
Company Ltd.,
Amber pint. 1950's.   **$10**

Left:
"PREMIER PORTER"
Brandon Brewing Co.,
Brandon, Manitoba.
Amber quart. Ca. 1919.
$35

Centre:
"THE EMPIRE BREWING CO. LTD.,
Brandon, Manitoba."
Aqua quart. BIMAL.
Early 1900's.   **$30**

Right:
"XXX PORTER"
The Empire Brewing Co.
Ltd., Brandon, Manitoba.
Amber quart. 1920's.
$35

Left to right:
"THE BRANDON BREWING CO."
Aqua pint. BIMAL.
Early 1900's.   **$15**

"THE BRANDON BREWING CO."
Amber pint. Ca. 1920's.
$15

"THE BRANDON BREWING CO."
Aqua pint.
Ca. 1920's.   **$10**

"THE EMPIRE BREWING CO."
Amber pint.
Ca. 1920's.   **$10**

"THE EMPIRE BREWING CO."
Aqua pint. BIMAL.
Ca. 1920's.   **$12**

Not Shown: **"THE EMPIRE BREWING CO."**
Clear pint. BIMAL.
Early 1900's.   **$15**

CARLINGS. Left to right:

"CARLING, LONDON"
Light amber. BIMAL.
1890's – early 1900's. **$40**

"STOUT FOR INVALIDS"
Amber pint. Early 1900's. **$25**

"AMBER ALE"
Amber pint. Early 1900's. **$15**

"AMBER ALE"
Green pint. Late 1920's. **$12**

"RED CAP ALE"
Green quart, with matching cap.
1940's. **$12**

"BLACK LABEL"
Clear pint. Late 1940's. **$8**

Left to right:
**"CARLING'S
BLACK LABEL"**
Clear pint. Late 1940's. **$10**

**"CARLING'S
RED CAP SPECIAL ALE"**
Green pint. 1940's. **$15**

"CARLING'S RED CAP"
Green pint. 1950's. **$7**

CARLING'S Left to right:

"OLD STOCK ALE"
Green pint. 1940-50. **$8**

"WHITE LABEL EXPORT ALE"
Green pint. Early 1950's. **$5**

"PILSENER" Amber pint. 1950's. **$4**

"EXPORT AMBER ALE" Green quart.
Late 1940's early 1950's. **$15**

"PORTER" Green pint. 1940 - 50. **$5**

"CARLING'S" Late 1950's early 1960's.
Left to right:
"BLACK LABEL" Clear pint. **$3**
"RED CAP ALE" Green pint. **$3**
"CINCI LAGER BEER" Clear pint. **$4**

"MAGNUM 5.5"
Carling-O'Keefe.
Stubby amber pint.
Late 1970's. Empty. **$3**

CHAMPLAIN BREWERY LTD.,
Quebec, Quebec. Left to right:

"TEMPERANCE PORTER"
Green pint. 1920's **$20**

"CHAMPLAIN SPECIAL"
Green quart. 1940's **$12**

"CHAMPLAIN PORTER"
Green quart. 1940's **$12**

"REAL STOUT"
Green pint. 1930's.**$15**

"CREAM PORTER"
Green quart with contents. 1940's. **$20**

**DORAN'S NORTHERN
BREWERY LTD.,** Port Arthur, Sudbury,
Sault-Ste. Marie and Timmins, Ontario.
Left to right:
"DORAN'S LAGER BEER"
Clear pint. late 1950's. **$8**

"DORAN'S NORTHERN ALE"
Green pint. Late 1950's. **$8**

"SILVER SPRAY BEER"
Clear pint. Late 1950's. **$8**

"SILVER FOAM LAGER"
Clear pint. Late 1950's. **$8**

**COPLAND BREWING CO.
LIMITED** Toronto, Ontario.

Left to right:

**EMBOSSED "Copland Brewing
Co. Limited, Toronto"**
Clear, BIMAL.
Ca. 1890's to early 1900's. **$40**

"COPLAND'S TONIC STOUT"
Green pint. 1940's. **$15**

"COPLAND'S STOCK ALE"
Green pint. 1940's. **$15**

"RED RIBBON BEER"
Green pint. 1940's. **$15**

"PAT'S STOCK ALE"
Green quart. 1940's. **$15**

**THE REINHARDT BREWING
CO. LTD.,** Toronto, Ontario.

Left:

**"REINHARDT & CO'S LAGER,
Toronto"** Mid amber, BIMAL.
Early 1900's. **$20**

Not Shown:

**"REINHARDT & CO'S LAGER,
Toronto"**Mid amber, BIMAL,
Crown closure. Ca. 1910. **$15**

Centre:

"WHITE HORSE ALE"
Green pint. 1940's. **$15**

Right:

"STOCK ALE"
Green quart. Late 1940's,
early 1950's. **$15**

DAWES BREWERY, Montreal, Quebec.

Left to right:

"BLACK HORSE ALE"
Green quart. Mid to late 1920's. **$20**

"BLACK HORSE PORTER"
Green quart. Mid to late 1920's. **$20**

"CREAM PORTER"
Green quart. 1930's. **$12**

"STOUT" Amber pint.
1940's. (Bottled for export). **$12**

"KINGSBEER LAGER"
Clear pint with matching cap.
1940's. **$10**

DAWES BREWERY,
Montreal, Quebec.

Left:

"CREAM PORTER"
Green quart. Early 1930's.
$20

Centre:

"CREAM PORTER"
Green pint. 1940's. **$15**

Right:

"BLACK HORSE ALE"
Green pint, non-returnable.
1940's. **$15**

FORMOSA SPRING BREWERY LIMITED, Formosa, Ontario

Left:
"OLD STOCK ALE"
Green pint. Late 1940's, early 1950's. **$9**

Centre:
"LUXURY PORTER"
Green pint. Late 1940's, early 1950's. **$9**

Right:
"MALTOSIA CREAM LAGER"
Clear pint. Late 1940's, early 1950's. **$9**

FORMOSA SPRING BREWERY LIMITED Left to right:

"CLUB BOCK BEER" Clear pint. 1950's. **$8**

"HUNT CLUB CREAM LAGER" Clear pint with contents. 1950's. **$10**

"TONIC STOUT" Green pint. 1950's. **$8**

"CLUB SELECT ALE" Green pint. 1950's. **$8**

Not Shown:
"HUNT CLUB CREAM LAGER" Clear pint, empty. 1950's. **$8.50**

FORT GARRY BREWERY LIMITED, Winnipeg, Manitoba.

Left -
"FRONTIER BEER"
Amber pint. 1950's. **$7**

Centre -
"FRONTIER BEER"
Amber pint.
Early 1950's. **$8**

Right -
"PILSENER"
Amber stubby pint.
Early 1950's. **$15**

Left to right:
"ALBERTA'S PRIDE"
Non-intoxicating. Lethbridge Breweries Ltd., Lethbridge, Alberta. Amber quart. Prohibition era. **$25**

"LETHBRIDGE PALE ALE"
Lethbridge Breweries Ltd. Amber pint. 1950's. **$10**

"BOHEMIAN MAID"
Bohemian Maid Brewing Co., Edmonton, Alberta.
Amber pint with matching cap. Late 1950's. **$10**

"EXTRA SPECIAL BEER"
North West Brewing Co., Edmonton, Alberta.
Amber pint. 1950's. **$10**

Left to right:

"SILVER FOAM PORTER"
The Sudbury Brewing & Malting
Co., Sudbury, Ontario.
Green pint. 1920's. **$15**

"DORAN'S CREAM LAGER"
Kakabeka Falls Brewing Co.,
Fort William, Ontario.
Clear pint with contents.
Late 1940's. **$15**

"KAKABEKA CREAM LAGER"
Kakabeka Falls Brewing Co.
Clear pint. Mid to late 1950's. **$8**

"SILVER FOAM BREW 57"
The Sudbury Brewing & Malting Co.
Clear pint. 1957 - 50th anniversary
of Sudbury Brewing. **$8**

ST LAWRENCE BREWERY LIMITED,
Cornwall, Ontario.
Left:
"PURE TABLE BEER"
Clear pint. Late 1920's. **$25**

Right:
"MILD TABLE BEER"
Clear pint. Late 1920's. **$25**

LABATT'S

Left:
"INDIA PALE ALE"
Bottled by Jas. McPharland,
341 King St., Kingston, Ontario.
Green pint. BIMAL. Late 1800's.
$50

Right:
"EXTRA STOCK ALE"
John Labatt, London, Canada.
"For 'foreign' export. Guaranteed
to keep 21 years."
Dark green pint. BIMAL.
Late 1800s.   **$30**

LABATT'S Left to right:
"OLD LONDON BREW"
Clear pint. 1920's.   **$15**

"CREMO LAGER"
Clear pint. 1920's.   **$12**

"EXTRA STOCK ALE"
Green quart. 1930's.   **$12**

"XXX STOUT"
Green pint. 1940's.   **$10**

"EXTRA STOCK ALE"
With Christmas label
"Season's Greetings."
Green pint. Late 1950's.   **$12**

LABATT'S. Left to right:
"INDIA PALE ALE"
Green pint, non-return-able. 1940's. **$7**

"CRYSTAL LAGER"
Clear pint. Late 1940's. **$10**

"INDIA PALE ALE"
Green pint with contents. 1940's. **$10**

"EXPORT INDIA PALE ALE"
Green pint with contents. 1950's. **$10**

"VELVET CREAM STOUT"
Green pint with contents. Late 1950's, early 1960's. **$8**

LABATT'S. Left to right:
"I P A" Green pint. Late 1950's. **$4**

"INDIA PALE ALE"
Green pint, non-returnable. Early 1950's. **$4**

"ANNIVERSARY ALE"
Green pint, non-returnable. Early 1950's. **$4**

"CRYSTAL BEER"
Clear pint. Late 1950's. **$6**

LABATT'S. Left to right:
"EXTRA STOCK ALE"
Clear pint with contents. 1955 - celebrating London's centennial. **$15**

"PILSENER" Green pint with contents. 1950's. **$9**

"ANNIVERSARY ALE" Green pint with contents. 1950's. **$7**

Left:
"LABATT'S EXTRA STOCK ALE"
"Brewed for the Coronation"
Elizabeth II, June, 1953.
Green pint in gold foil.
With contents. **$20**

Right:
"LABATT'S ROYAL BLUE"
"Celebrating 100 Years Service,
The Royal Canadian Regiment,
1883 - 1983" Amber pint. Gold
lettering and border on royal blue
label. Sold at London, Ontario only
for about three weeks.
With contents. **$6**

KUNTZ BREWERY LIMITED,
Waterloo, Ontario. 1920's - 1930's.

Left to right:

"OLDE FRIAR STOUT" Green pint. **$12 - $15**

EMBOSSED
"Return this bottle to
L. Kuntz Park Brewery
Waterloo" Embossed
"Waterloo" on base.
Slightly sun-cast.
Ht. 10 1/4" Ca. 1908.
$60

"YE OLDE INN ALE" Amber pint. **$12 - $15**

"YE OLDE DUTCH LAGER" Clear pint.**$12 - $15**

"YE OLDE INN ALE" Green pint. **$12 - $15**

KUNTZ BREWERY LIMITED.

Left:

"OLD TAVERN LAGER"
Clear pint. 1940's. **$8**

Centre:

"OLDE FRIAR STOUT"
Green pint. 1940's. **$10**

Right -

**"KUNTZ'S OLDE
TAVERN ALE"**
Green pint. 1940's. **$10**

Not Shown:

**"THE ORIGINAL
KUNTZ'S LAGER"**
Clear pint. 1940's. **$10**

LUCKY LAGER BREWING CO.,
New Westminister, B.C.

Left: **"YE OLDE ALE"**
Amber pint. 1950's. **$7**

Right: **"LUCKY LAGER"**
Amber pint. 1950's. **$7**

VANCOUVER BREWERIES LTD.,
Vancouver, B.C.

Left: **"PILSENER LAGER BEER"**
Amber pint. 1940's. **$10**

Right: **"U.B.C. BOHEMIAN"**
Amber pint. 1940's. **$10**

Left to right :
"RAINIER PALE ALE" Westminster Brewery Ltd., New Westminster, B.C.
Clear pint. 1940's. **$15**

"BRITANNIA BEER" Westminster Brewery Ltd.
Clear pint. 1940's. **$15**

"BANKERS BURTON TYPE ALE"
Lucky Lager Brewing Co., New Westminster, B.C.
Green pint. 1950's. **$10**

MOLSON'S. Left to right:

"XXX PORTER"
Amber split. 1920's. **$15**

"EXPORT ALE"
Green quart. 1940's. **$15**

"STOCK ALE"
Green pint. Early 1940's. **$10**

"INDIA PALE ALE"
Green quart with matching cap.
Late 1940's. **$12**

"CREAM PORTER"
Green quart with contents.
Early 1950's. **$15**

MOLSON'S. Left to right:
"CREAM PORTER" Green pint with contents. Late 1940's. **$15**
"EXPORT ALE" Green quart. Mid 1940's. **$8**
"EXPORT ALE" Green pint with contents, non-returnable. 1940's. **$12**
"PILSNER BEER" Amber pint. 1950's. **$10**

Beers with labels to commemorate an event

VALUE $4+ EACH

Left:
"RUDOLPH & BEGG BR'G CO. LTD., St. Thomas, Ont."
Mid amber pint. ABM.
Early 1900's.**$45**

Centre:
"BOWIE & CO. BREWERY LIMITED,
Brockville, Ont."
Green quart with contents.
BIMAL. Early 1900's. **$60**

Right:
"BOWIE & CO. BREWERY LIMITED, Brockville, Ont."
Green pint. BIMAL.
Early 1900's. **$50**

Bottles and six-pack case from the new Sleeman brewery. Clear, embossed with company logo, beaver and maple leaf, paper neck labels indicate type of beer.

THE SLEEMAN BREWING & MALTING CO. LTD., Guelph, Ontario. 1834-1933.

Reopened August, 1988 by John W. Sleeman, great-great grandson of the founder John H. Sleeman.

Products are brewed according to the family's original recipes using traditional brewing methods. Sleeman's brewing capacity is 30 million bottles a year.

Sleeman's 19% owned by Stroh Brewery, Detroit, Michigan, will be making and distributing Stroh's beers in Canada. Using Stroh's recipes, Sleeman's will be the first Canadian company to brew an authentic American beer in Canada. Sleeman's products, Cream Ale, Silver Creek Lager and Stout, will be distributed in the U.S. by Stroh's.

"SLEEMAN'S EXPORT LAGER" (Guelph, Ont.)
Dark amber pint. BIMAL.
Early 1900's. **$75**

Left to right :

"JAMES READY, St. John, N.B."
Clear split. Ca. 1900. **$20**

"JAMES READY BREWER,
St. John, N.B."
Clear split. Ca. 1900. **$20**

"JAMES READY BREWERIES LTD.,
St. John, N.B."
Clear split. Teens - Ca. 1920's. **$15**

"READY'S BREWERIES LIMITED,
St. John, N.B."
Aqua split. Teens - Ca. 1920's. **$15**

Left:
"TEN-PENNY OLD STOCK ALE"
New Brunswick Brewery,
Fairville & St. John, N.B.
Green quart. 1940's **$15**

Centre:
"MOOSEHEAD PALE ALE"
Moosehead Breweries Ltd.,
Lancaster, N.B.
Green pint with contents.
Late 1950's. **$12**

Right -
"MOOSEHEAD PALE ALE"
Green quart. 1950's. **$15**

Left to right:

"MOOSEHEAD LONDON STOUT"
Moosehead Breweries Limited,
Lancaster, N.B.
Green pint. Early 1950's. **$10**

"MOOSEHEAD PALE ALE"
New Brunswick Brewery,
Fairville, N.B.
Clear quart. 1940's. **$15**

"STAG'S HEAD CANADIAN ALE"
Alexander Keith & Sons Ltd.,
Halifax, N.S.
Green quart. 1940's. **$12**

"OLAND'S EXTRA STOUT"
Oland & Son Limited, Halifax, N.S.
Green pint. Late 1950's. **$8**

Left:

"ALPINE LAGER BEER"
Moosehead Breweries Ltd.,
Lancaster, N.B.
Clear pint with contents.
Late 1950's. **$12**

Centre:

**"MOOSEHEAD
PALE ALE"**
Moosehead Breweries Ltd.
Green pint with contents.
Late 1950's. **$12**

Right:

"INDIA PALE ALE"
Alexander Keith & Son.,
Halifax, N.S.
Green pint. 1930 - 40. **$10**

OLAND & SON, Halifax, N.S.

Left:
"OLANDS ALE"
Green pint. 1950's. **$15**

Right -
"BAVARIAN LAGER"
Clear quart. 1950's. **$15**

"O'MALLEY ALE" O'Malley Brewery, Quebec, Quebec.
Amber pint. 1965. **$10**
Established 1965, business failed, only brewed two batches of beer.

RED BALL BREWERY LTD., St. John, N.B. Left to right:
"ARCTIC CANADIAN ALE." Clear pint. 1930's. **$15**
"OLD STOCK PALE ALE" Clear pint. 1940's. **$15**
"EXTRA STOCK ALE" Green quart. 1940's. **$15**
"CABOT ALE" Green pint. Late 1940's, early 1950's. **$10**
"OLD SCOTCH ALE" Green pint. Late 1940's, early 1950's. **$10**

O'KEEFE'S. Left to right:

"IMPERIAL LAGER"
Green pint. 1930's - 40's. **$12**

"EXTRA OLD STOCK ALE"
Green quart. Late 1920's. **$12**

"EXTRA OLD STOCK ALE"
Green pint with matching cap.1953
Coronation label - St. James Palace. **$8**

"OLD VIENNA"
Clear pint. Mid 1950's. **$7**

"DOUBLE STOUT"
Green pint. Late 1950's. **$7**

O'KEEFE'S.
Six pack with empties.
Red and blue on plain carton.
1950's. **$50**

Left to right:

**"O'KEEFE'S EXTRA OLD
STOCK ALE"**1953 Coronation label -
Big Ben. Green pint. **$5**

"O'KEEFE ALE"
Green pint. 1950's. **$5**

O'KEEFE'S. Left to right:

"OLD VIENNA BEER" Clear pint. 1950's. **$7**

"OLD VIENNA BEER" Clear pint. Late 1950's. **$5**

"DOUBLE STOUT" Green pint. 1950's. **$8**

"BLENDED OLD STOCK ALE" Amber pint. 1960's. **$2**

Left to right:

"PELLER'S PREMIUM STOUT"
Peller Brewing Company, Hamilton, Ontario.
Green pint with contents. 1950's. **$15**
"HIGH LIFE"
Premier Brewing Co. Ltd., Brandon, Man.
Clear pint. 1950's. **$15**

"PALE ALE" Port Hope
Brewing & Malting Co.,
Port Hope, Ont.
Green quart. Ca. 1900.
$25

Left:
"COLBERT,
 Egmondville" (Ontario)
Amber, Ht. 11 1/2".
1890's. **$125**

Right:
**"RETURN TO EGMONDVILLE
BREWING CO."**
Clear. Ca. 1910. **$100**

Left to right:
"ROYAL EXPORT BOCK BEER"
Kootenay Breweries Ltd.,
Nelson and Trail, B.C.
Amber pint. Late 1940's, early 1950's.
$15

**"SILVER SPRING BREW
BOCK BEER"**
Pheonix Brewing Co., Victoria, B.C.
Amber pint. Late 1940's. **$15**

"OLD DUBLIN ALE"
Princeton Brewing Co. Ltd.,
Princeton, B.C.
Amber pint. Early 1950's. **$10**

"TARTAN LAGER BEER"
Tartan Brewing Co. Ltd.,
Prince George, B.C.
Amber pint. Early 1970's. **$8**

Left to right:

"RIEDLE'S EXPORT BEER"
The Riedle Brewery Limited,
Winnipeg, Manitoba.
Clear pint with matching cap.
1940's. **$12**

"GRANT'S TIP TOP LAGER"
Grant's Brewery Ltd., Winnipeg,
Manitoba. Amber pint.
Mid 1950's. **$12**

**"RIEDLE & GRANT'S
5 STAR LAGER BEER"**
Amber pint with matching cap.
Mid 1950's. **$12**

"WHITE LABEL BEER"
The Kiewel Brewery Co. Ltd.,
St. Boniface, Manitoba.
Clear pint. Early 1940's. On reverse
of label "Buy War Savings Certificates
for Victory." **$12**

"COUNTRY CLUB"
Pelissier's Brewery Limited,
Winnipeg, Manitoba.
Clear pint with matching cap.
1940's. **$12**

SASKATOON BREWING CO. LTD., Saskatoon, Sask. Left to right:

"BAVARIAN CLUB" Amber pint. 1950's. **$10**

"RED RIBBON" Amber pint. Golden anniversary 1906 - 1956. **$10**

"BIG CHIEF BEER" Amber pint with matching cap. 1950's. **$12**

"BIG CHIEF STOUT" Amber pint. 1950's. **$10**

SASKATOON BREWING CO. LTD.

Left: **"RED RIBBON BEER"**
Amber pint with contents.
1950's. **$15**

Right: **"BAVARIAN CLUB"**
Amber pint with contents.
1950's. **$15**

BLUE LABEL BREWING LTD.,
Regina, Saskatchewan.

Left: **"LAGER BEER"**
Amber pint with contents. 1950's. **$15**

Right: **"BLUE LABEL BEER"**
Amber pint. 1950's. **$10**

Above - left to right:

"McDONAGH & SHEA, Winnipeg, Man."
Aqua pint, BIMAL. Early 1900's. **$20**

"McDONAGH & SHEA, Winnipeg, Man."
Amber pint. ABM. Ca. 1920's. **$12**

"SHEA'S FINE OLD STOCK ALE"
Shea's Winnipeg Brewery Ltd.
Amber pint. Late 1940's. **$10**

"SHEA'S SELECT BEER"
Shea's Winnipeg Brewery Ltd.
Clear pint. Late 1940's. **$10**

Left to right:

"SHEA'S STOUT"
Shea's Winnipeg Brewery Ltd.
Amber pint with contents. 1940's.
$15

"SHEA'S SELECT BEER"
Shea's Winnipeg Brewery Ltd.
Amber pint. 1940's.
$10

SICK'S (Edmonton & Lethbridge) BREWERIES. 1950's.

Left to right:

"PILSNER STYLE"Amber pint. **$12**

"EDMONTON EXPORT"Amber pint. **$8**

"LETHBRIDGE EXPORT"Amber pint. **$8**

"OLD BOHEMIAN" Sick's Prince Albert Brewery Ltd.
Amber pint with contents. 1950's. **$15**

SICK'S (Regina & Prince Albert) BREWERIES. 1950's.

Left to right:

"OLD BOHEMIAN" Amber pint. **$10**

"YE OLD ENGLISH NUT BROWN ALE" Amber pint. **$12**

"PILSNER" Amber pint. **$10**

Left: **"BIG HORN STOUT"** Dow Brewery (Western) Ltd., Calgary, Alberta. Amber pint. Early 1960's. **$10**

Right: **"BIG HORN BRAND BEER"** Big Horn Brewing Co. Ltd., Calgary, Alberta. Amber pint. Late 1950's. **$10**

Left to right:

"ACE LAGER" Capilano Brewing
Co., Vancouver, B.C.
Clear pint. 1930's. **$20**

"REVELSTOKE 3X PALE BEER"
Enterprise Brewery,
Revelstoke, B.C.
Clear pint. Late 1930's,
early 1940's. **$15**

"FERNIE BEER"
Fernie Brewing Co., Fernie, B.C.
Amber pint. 1950's. **$10**

"EXPORT LAGER"
Victoria Pheonix Brewing Co.,
Victoria, B.C.
Amber pint. 1940's. **$15**

Left to right: Amber pints. 1950's. **Each $8 – $10**

"CARIBOU LAGER" Caribou Brewing Co., Ltd., Prince George, B.C.

"HIGH LIFE" Caribou Brewing Co. Ltd.

"COLUMBIA LAGER" Interior Breweries Ltd., Nelson, B.C.

"PALE KOOTENAY ALE" Interior Breweries Ltd., Creston, B.C.

"OKANAGAN LAGER" Enterprise Brewery Ltd., Revelstoke, B.C.

Breweriana "Go-Withs"

Government regulations regarding advertising did not allow the brewing industry to use the media to promote their beverages, therefore, they promoted their products in the licensed premises that served beer using numerous methods. Promotional items used to advertise the many brands of beer and ale available include ashtrays; tip and serving trays; posters; signs; calendars; thermometers; bottle openers; coasters; salt shakers; mirrors; clocks; key rings; playing cards and glasses.

Regulations regarding point of sale advertising have changed over the years and many of the types of advertising previously used by the breweries are no longer found in licensed establishments.

Today collectors of breweriana seek all of the many forms of advertising and promotional items to add to their collection of bottles and cans.

"LETHBRIDGE BREWING & MALTING CO. LTD."
"Good Morning" By American Art Works, Coshocton. 15" x 15" **$1,000**

ELECTRIC CLOCK "CANADA BUD"

Reverse screen on glass, red ground. Clock in going order. 10" x 18" 1930's. **$350**

CLOCK DIAL "ASK FOR LABATT'S"

Clock by Shonbeck Clock Co., Hamilton, Ontario. Diam. 16" **$75**

"BIERE O'KEEFE ALE"

Internally lit sign with electric clock. Length 24" 1940's. **$65**

"CARLING RED CAP ALE"

Internally lit sign. Length 24" 1940's. **$65**

STATUE "Dawes Black Horse Brewery"
Marked "Ross Butler" Ht. 19" Length of base 18 1/2"   **$450**

"EDWARD L. DREWRY"
Metal sign, 11" x 14"   **$350**

MATCH SCRATCH CARDS
Left: "Dominion Brewery Co."
4 1/2" x 9 1/2"   **$50**
Right: "Molson's"
4 1/2" x 9 1/2" Mint.   **$100**

Left:
"KUNTZ'S"
Full colour metal sign.   **$700**

Right:
"SILVER SPRING ALE"
Enamel on tin sign.
11" x 17" 1940's.   **$60**

"SILVER SPRING ALE"
Enamel on tin sign. 9" x 9 1/2" 1940's.   **$25**

"WALKERVILLE BREWERY"
Picture under glass" 12 1/2" x 18". **$75**

"BRADING'S CINCI" Composition
"Handsome Waiter." Red lettering on
black base. Ht. 16". **$40**

"O'KEEFE'S" Full colour tin sign.
11" x 14" Ca. 1910. **$500**

"CANADA BUD" Full colour porcelain enamel on
metal sign. 10" x 16" 1940's. **$250**

"JOHN H. R. MOLSON & BROS."
Semicircular enamel sign.
15" x 24" Very scarce. **$750**

"RIVERSIDE BEER AND ALE"
11" x 17" Ca. 1927 – 35. **$750**

"BAJUS" Metal sign, 7" x 10" Ca. 1910. **$400**

Tip/Change Trays

Small round, square or rectangular trays used by waiters to return change to customers. The brewing industry was restricted by government regulations regarding advertising of their products and tip/change trays were one method brewers used to promote their brands.

Prices listed are for trays in near mint or mint condition.

TIP TRAYS Left to right:

"BRADING'S"	$50 - $100
"KUNTZ'S"	$100 - $200
"HUETHER'S"	$100 - $200

TIP TRAYS Left to right:

"CARLING'S"	$30 - $50
"DAWE'S BREWERY"	$50 - $100
"KUNTZ'S"	$30 - $50

SKUCE CARTOONS ON TIP TRAYS Left to right:

"CANADA BUD" Ontario workers, factories and farm.   **$50 - $100**

"CAPITAL" Two Tourists.   **$100 - $200**

"CANADA BUD" Lady and Gentleman.   **$50 - $100**

TIP TRAYS Left to Right :

"BRADING'S"	**$50 - $100**
"DOMINION"	**$100 - $200**
"COSGRAVE'S"	**$100 - $200**

TIP TRAYS Left to right:

"HOFER BREWING"	**$100 - $200**
"DREWRY'S"	**$100 - $200**
"BRITISH AMERICAN" Handsome Waiter.	**$50 - $100**

TIP TRAYS Left to right:

"DOW"	$30 - $50
"CHAMPLAIN"	$50 - $100
"SILVER SPIRE" (Taylor & Bate's)	$50 - $100

TIP TRAYS Left to right:

"KUNTZ'S"	$100 - $200
"TAYLOR & BATE'S"	$200 - $300
"BIXEL'S"	$200 - $300

TIP TRAYS Left to right:

"WALKERVILLE BREWERY"	$100 - $200
"WALKERVILLE BREWERY"	$100 - $200
"WALKERVILLE BREWERY"	$100 - $200

Serving Trays

Serving trays, a method of advertising used by breweries to promote their products, were used in licensed premises across Canada. They are now among the most popular items of breweriana collected today.

Trays were made in the United States, England and Canada using several types of material – nickel plated steel; porcelain enamel; aluminum; brass; lithographed tin and plastic.

Prices listed are for trays in near mint or mint condition.

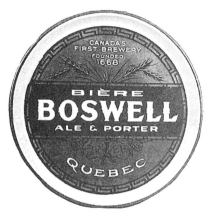

"BOSWELL" $50 - $100

"BOSWELL'S" $50 - $100

"BRADING'S" $50 - $100

"BRITISH AMERICAN" $50 - $100

"CALGARY BREWING"
$100 - $200

"CANADA BUD"
$100 - $200

"CANADA BUD"
$100 - $200

"CANADA BUD"
$50 - $100

"CHAMPLAIN"
$100 - $200

"COSGRAVE'S"
$100 - $200

"CAPITAL"
$100 - $200

"CAPITAL"
$200 - $300

Left:

"CAPITAL" $300 - $400

NOTE: No reference to beer on this tray. Thought to have been issued in 1923 to celebrate the opening of the Parliament buildings in Ottawa which were destroyed by fire Feb. 3, 1916.

"CAPITAL"
$100 - $200

"CARLING'S"
$50 - $100

"CARLING'S" $50 - $100

"DAWES" $300 - $400

"DAWES" $50 - $100

"DAWES" $30 - $50

"DAWES" $300 - $400

"DOMINION" $100 - $200

"DOW" $30 - 50

"DREWRYS" $200 - $300

"EKERS" $400 - $500
Note: Tray illustrated has been restored.
Value $200

"EKERS" $100 - $200

"FRONTENAC" $75 - $150

"HUETHER'S" $50 - $100

"KUNTZ'S BREWERY"
$100 - $200

"KUNTZ'S BREWERY" $500+

"LABATT'S" $30 - $50

"LABATT'S" $30 - $50

"LABATT'S" $30 - $50

"MOLSON" $30 - $50

"MOLSON'S" $50 - $100

"MOLSON" $15

"O'KEEFE'S" $50 - $100

"RED BALL" $300 - $400

"REINHARDT'S"
$100 - $200

"RIVERSIDE"
$400 - $500

"SUDBURY BREWING"
$200 - $300

"SILVER SPRING"
$50 - $100

"TAYLOR & BATE'S"
$100 - $200

"WALKERVILLE BREWERY"
$100 - $200

"WESTMINSTER BREWERY" $500+

Ash Trays

Ash trays are another popular breweriana collectable. They are made in many styles, round, square, hexagonal, triangular and rectangular and lettered with brewery names and brands.

Below left: **"MOLSON'S"** Solid brass. **$30**

Below right: **"BOSWELL'S"** Solid brass. **$30**

"DAWES BLACK HORSE"
Solid brass. Only one known. **$150**

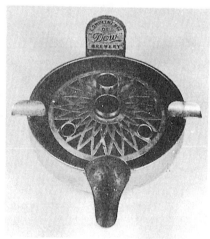

Above:

"COMPLIMENTS OF DOW BREWERY"
Nickel plated, made in England. Patent No. 190884. Sold by J.R. Gaunt Ltd., Montreal. Grill over tray, two cigarette snuffers, one cigar snuffer, pipe cleaner missing. **$100**

Left: **"CAPITAL ALE"**
Brown and cream glazed pottery. Also found in blue and green. **$50**

ASH TRAYS - PAINTED ON TIN Left to right:

"BRADING'S"	**$25**
"CAPITAL"	**$25**
"REGAL"	**$25**

ASH TRAYS - PORCELAIN ENAMEL Left to Right:

"WALKERVILLE"	**$20**
"WALKERVILLE"	**$20**
"MOLSON'S"	**$10**

ASH TRAYS - PORCELAIN ENAMEL Left to right:

"DAWES BLACK HORSE"	**$15**
"DAWES BLACK HORSE"	**$30**
"DAWES BLACK HORSE"	**$10**

ASH TRAYS Left to right:

"BRADING'S" Metal	**$15**
"BRADING'S" Glass	**$10**
"BRADING'S" Metal	**$10**

"SILVER FOAM" (Sudbury Brewing & Malting)
Ash tray by Medalta Pottery, Medicine Hat, Alberta.   **$100**

ASH TRAYS Left to right:

"CARLING'S" Glass	$100
"FORNTENAC" Aluminum	$60
"REINHARDT'S" Glass	$100

GLASS ASH TRAYS Left to right:

"BRADING'S"	$8
"BRITISH AMERICAN"	$8
"CANADA BUD"	$8
"O'KEEFE'S"	$8

METAL ASH TRAYS Left to right:

"KUNTZ'S" (chipped)	$12
"REGAL"	$15
"SILVER SPIRE" (Taylor & Bates)	$15

ASH TRAYS – PORCELAIN ENAMEL Left to right:

"DOMINION"	**$60**
"BLACK PIRATE ALE" (British American)	**$60**
"COSGRAVES"	**$40**
"KUNTZ'S"	**$60**
"REGAL"	**$60**

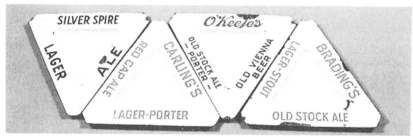

ASH TRAYS – PORCELAIN ENAMEL Left to right:

"SILVER SPIRE" (Taylor & Bates)	**$40**
"CARLING'S"	**$40**
"O'KEEFE'S"	**$40**
"BRADING'S"	**$40**

ASH TRAYS – METAL Left to right:

"BIXEL'S"	**$20**
"BRITISH AMERICAN"	**$15**
"FRONTENAC"	**$12**

ASH TRAYS – METAL Left to right:

"CANADA BUD"	**$15**
"CARLING'S"	**$15**
"HEUTHER'S"	**$15**

Beer Bottle Openers

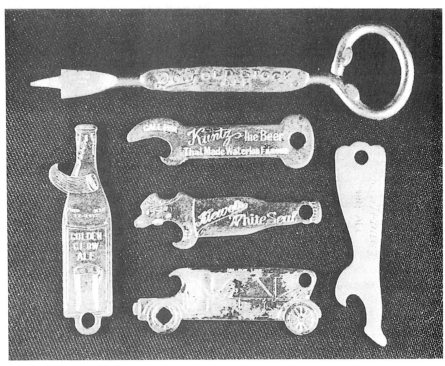

BOTTLE OPENERS. Metal, early 1900's.

Top to bottom: Dow, length 6"; Kuntz'; Kiewel's; Drewry's.

Left: Pellisier, patented Mar. 12, 1912.

Right: Frontenac.

Each $20

Left:
BOTTLE OPENERS.
With wood handles.
L. 4 1/4" to 4 3/4"
Each $10

LABATT'S ROCKER STYLE BOTTLE OPENERS.
Plastic and metal. Only brewery to use this style of opener, 1960's. L. 5"
Each $5

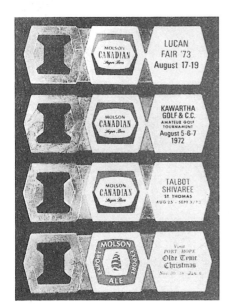
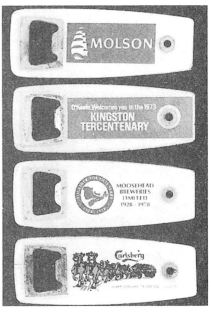

SPECIAL EVENT OPENERS.
Plastic and metal. 1970's. L. 5"
Each $2 - $3

BOTTLE OPENERS
Plastic and metal. 1970's. L. 4 1/2"
Each $2

Beer Bottle Caps

Beer bottle caps illustrated in this section are all cork lined.

Values:

Cork lined (discontinued 1960/61)   **$1**
Prices are higher for unusual and scarce bottle caps.

Plastic lined   **.50**
Prices are higher for limited edition or special occasion caps.

Dairy Bottles

Commercial delivery of milk in bottles began just over one hundred years ago. The milk bottle patented by Dr. Hervey D. Thatcher in 1884, although not the first milk bottle patented in the United States, was the first commercially successful milk container.

Milk bottles were sealed with lightening type closures until about 1900 when a type of bottle was designed that could be sealed with a paper or cardboard cap.

During the 1920's Canadian dairies began using the cream top bottles and the square milk bottle came into use during the 1950's in Canada.

Most milk bottles found today are clear. Amber coloured bottles were used by some dairies, amber being a colour that would protect the contents from light. Consumers preferred to buy milk in clear glass bottles and therefore dairies discontinued the use of amber bottles.

Dairy bottles were marked with the dairy's name and other information in three ways:

EMBOSSED. Dairy name in raised script or print, sometimes with instructions or slogans such as "Wash and Return" – "Purity, Quality & Cleanliness Guaranteed." Some dairy bottles were also ribbed or decorated with maple leaves, flowers and cows etc.

APPLIED COLOURED LABELS. A labeling process developed in the United States during the 1920's which came into popular use during the 1930's on milk and soft drink bottles. A paste made of borasilicate, oil and a colouring oxide was applied to bottles through a steel screen. The labeled bottle then had to be baked at a temperature of about 300 degrees Fahrenheit. If the label consisted of two colours the first colour applied had to dry before the next one could be added.
A slow and expensive process. In the 1940's it was discovered that by using a plastic resin in place of the oil in the mixture, drying time between applications of colour was almost eliminated, thus speeding the process and making it a more common procedure.

PAPER LABELS. Also were used by some dairies on plain or embossed bottles.

Embossed Dairy Bottles

Above - Left to right -

"ABSOLUTELY PURE MILK - THE MILK PROTECTOR" Patented by Dr. Hervey Dexter Thatcher, Potsdam, New York.

Quart, stippled cow, lightning type closure. **$400**

"ABSOLUTELY PURE MILK - THE MILK PROTECTOR" On reverse "A.A. Barnhart"

Quart, cow not stippled.   **$500+**

Note: It has been reported that a Canadian, Albert Augustus Barnhart, invented, but did not patent this type of bottle. It is possible that the bottle in the middle was made in Canada, but it is not known if this type of milk bottle was ever used by a Canadian dairy.

"CITY OF BELLVILLE MILK COMPANY,

Trade Mark OK Registered Limited"

Quart. **$350**

Left:

"ABSOLUTELY PURE MILK" On reverse, "Thatcher's Dairy Bottle Pat'd. 1884" Reproduction, marked on base "Made in Italy" and "Crowford China Company."

Pale blue, also comes in amber and clear. **$25**

"SCOTIA PURE MILK CO. LTD., Halifax, N.S." Left to right:

Quart, amber bowling pin. Early 1900's. Only 2 known. **$350**

Pint, Pottery. Only 3 known. **$350**

Quart, suncast. **$100**

Quart, gray glass bowling pin. **$75**

Not Shown:
AMBER QUART
Bowling pin shape.
No embossing. **$75**

"OTTAWA DAIRY CO., Ottawa, Ont."
Amber half-pint. **$300**

Left:
"ASHBY BROS DAIRY.
Believed to be a Toronto dairy.
Clear pint. **$300+**

Right:
"PURE MILK CORPORATION LIMITED, Hamilton, Ont."
Amber quart. **$175**

"SCOTIA DAIRY" Ottawa, Ont.
Quart. Only one known.
No value available.

"F & G MARKETS" (Fitzpatrick &
Garrity) Peterborough, Ont.
Quart. **$20**

Left to Right -
"SUNSHINE DAIRY" North Bay, Ont.
Quart. **$25**

"PALM DAIRIES" Edmonton, Alberta.
Quart. **$20**

"PURITY DAIRIES LIMITED"
(The name Purity appears on bottles
from several provinces and could be
a franchise or co-operative).
Quart. **$25**

Left to right:

"MAPLE LEAF DAIRY"
Oshawa, Ont.
Quart **$50**

**"PURE MILK
COMPANY"**
Oshawa, Ont.
Quart **$50**

"OSHAWA DAIRY"
Quart **$20**

Left to right:
"CITY DAIRY"
Toronto, Ont.
A Borden's quart with
diamond collar. **$15**

"FISHER'S DAIRY"
Cobourg, Ont.
Pint **$35**

**"CORNWALL'S EAST SIDE
DAIRY CO."** Cornwall, Ont.
Quart **$20**

Left to right:
"PICKERING DAIRY" Pickering, Ont.
Half-pint **$60**

"GRANDY'S DAIRY" Whitby, Ont.
Quart **$95**

"CEDARDALE DAIRY" Orono, Ont.
Quart **$75**

**"BEATON'S DAIRY
PRODUCTS LTD."** Oshawa, Ont.
Pint **$45**

Left to right:
"FRASEA FARMS LTD." Quart **$15**
"LINDSAY CREAMERY LIMITED" Quart **$45**
"PRODUCERS DAIRY" Quart **$15**

Left to right:
"THUNDER BAY CO-OP DAIRY LTD."
Thunder Bay, Ont.
Quart **$20**

"HUNTSVILLE DAIRY"
Huntsville, Ont.
Quart **$30**

"LAKEFIELD DAIRY"
Lakefield, Ont.
Quart **$50**

Left to right:
"DUNVILLE DAIRY"
Dunville, Ont.
Quart **$12**

"PRICE'S"
Kingston, Ont.
Pint **$12**

"BLUE RIBBON DAIRY"
Quart **$20**

"PETERBORO MILK PRODUCTS LTD." Left to right:

Quarter-pint **$30**   Half-pint **$25**

Pint **$25**   Quart **$25**

Left to right:

"OTTAWA DAIRY CO. LIMITED" Ottawa, Ont.   Half-pint **$25**

"OTTAWA DAIRY CO. LIMITED" Ottawa, Ont.   Pint **$20**

"OTTAWA DAIRY CO" Ottawa, Ont.   Quart **$15**

Left:
"CASWELL DAIRY"
Simcoe, Ont.
Quart, pint and half-pint.
Set $50

Left to right:
"JAMES SINNOT"
Port Hope, Ont.
Ribbed Quart **$25**

"JAMES SINNOT"
Port Hope, Ont.
Ribbed Pint **$25**

"JAMES SINNOT"
Port Hope, Ont.
Half-pint **$20**

Left to right:
"MONTREAL COTTON CO."
Valleyfield, Que.
Pint **$20**

"LAITERIE ST. ALEXANDRE LTEE." Longueil, Que.
Quart **$30**

"JERSEY ISLAND DAIRY"
Danforth Ave., Toronto, Ont.
Pint **$150**

Left to right:

"SANITARY DAIRY LIMITED" Quart **$15**

"SILVER SPRINGS DAIRY FARM" Ottawa, Ont. Quart **$25**

"PETERBORO D.B.A." **(Dairy Bottle Association)** Quart **$20**

Left to right:

"SHERBROOKE PURE MILK COMPANY" Quart **$15**

"ELMHURST DAIRY LIMITED" Montreal, Que. Quart **$20**

"KORMAN'S DAIRY LIMITED" Timmins, Ont. Quart **$20**

Above left: **"WILLARD'S"** Toronto, Ont.
Cream top. Pint. **$150**

Above right: **"SILVERWOOD'S
SAFE MILK"** Pint. **$250**

"SILVERWOOD'S"
Cream top. Quart **$100**
Cream ladle **$15**

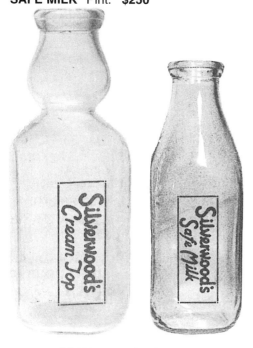

Above left: **"SILVERWOOD'S CREAM TOP"**
Applied coloured label. Quart. **$100**

Above right: **"SILVERWOOD'S SAFE MILK"**
Applied coloured label. Quart. **$15**

CREAM TOP
Quart with
cream ladle. **$25**

Left to right:

"ORILLIA DAIRY CO." Orillia, Ont. Quart   **$45**

"HIGHFIELD DAIRY" Port Hope, Ont. Quart.   **$20**

"OWEN SOUND DAIRY CO. LTD." Owen Sound, Ont. Quart.   **$15**

"WILSON'S"Trenton, Ont. Quart.   **$15**

Left to right:
"HAMILTON DAIRIES LTD." Hamilton, Ont. Quart. **$20**

"KIRKLAND LAKE STORE BOTTLE" Kirkland Lake, Ont. Pint.   **$30**

"SMITH FALLS DAIRY" Smith Falls, Ont. Half-pint.   **$25**

Left to right:

"B.C. & S. Co." Brandon, Man. (Brandon Creamery & Supply Co.)
Pint. **$30**

"B.C. & S. Co." Brandon, Man. Quart. **$30**

"WINNIPEG PURE MILK CO."
Winnipeg, Man. Pint. **$35**

Left to right:

"MARTIN DAIRY PRODUCTS LTD." Welland, Ont. Pint. **$12**

"SUTTON DAIRY" Sutton, Ont. Pint. **$25**

"SUTTON DAIRY & CREAMERY LTD." Sutton West, Ont. Pint. **$30**

"IDEAL DAIRY" Peterborough, Ont. Pint. **$30**

Left to right:

"LAURENTIA" Quarter-pint **$35**

"LAURENTIA" Half-pint **$20**

"LAURENTIA MILK CO." Battleford, Sask. Pint. **$35**

"LAURENTIA MILK CO." Red Deer, Alberta. Quart. **$30**

NOTE: Dairy bottles with paper labels intact and complete are scarce.

Left:
"LAURENTIA MILK CO."
41 Lombard St.,
Toronto, Ont.
Half-pint. **$35**

Right:
"LAURENTIA"
Pint. **$15**

Left to right:
"J. ZUKER" Toronto, Ont.
Pint. **$40**

"GLENWOOD FARM DAIRIES" Canton, Ont.
Half-pint. **$45**

"SUNSHINE DAIRY"
Peterborough or London, Ont.
Pint. **$25**

Left to right:
"MAPLE LEAF DAIRY LIMITED" Ottawa, Ont.
Pint. **$25**

"P. CLARKE SILVER SPRINGS DAIRY"
Ottawa, Ont.
Pint. **$20**

"PETERSON"
Almonte, Ont.
Pint. **$15**

Left to right:
"CO-OPERATIVE MILK BOTTLE ASSOCIATION"
St. John, N.B.
Half-pint. **$20**

"PURITY MILK REG."
St. John, N.B.
Half-pint. **$20**

"FARMERS DAIRY"
St. John, N.B.
Half-pint. **$20**

Left to right:
"KINGSTON MILK DIS-TRIBUTORS"
Kingston, Ont.
Half-pint. **$15**

"FARMERS DAIRY"
Toronto, Ont.
Pint. **$15**

"CITY DAIRY CO. LIMITED" Toronto, Ont.
Pint. **$10**

Left to right:
"MONTROSE"
Belleville, Ont.
Pint. **$12**

"RITCHIE'S DAIRY LIMITED"
Toronto, Ont.
Pint. **$25**

"TORONTO DAIRY CO." 77 Osborne St.,
Toronto, Ont.
Pint. **$35**

Left to right:
"IDEAL DAIRY"
Half-pint. **$50**

"GLENRAE DAIRY"
R.R. Stevens,
Bowmanville, Ont.
Pint. **$75**

"OSHAWA-WHITBY-BOWMANVILLE MILK BOTTLE ASSOCIATION"
Half-pint. **$20**

Left to right:
"OTTAWA MILK BOTTLE ASSOCIATION LIMITED"
Ottawa, Ont.
Pint. **$15**

"KINCARDINE DAIRY"
Murray Bros.,
Kincardine, Ont.
Pint. **$15**

"MAPLE LEAF DAIRY"
Ridgetown, Ont.
Pint. **$30**

Left to right:
"J.J. JOUBERT LIMITEE"
Pint. **$10**

"CREMERIE DES TROIS RIVIERES LTEE."
Trois Rivieres, Que.
Pint. **$10**

"FARMERS LIMITED"
Halifax, N.S.
Pint. **$15**

Left to right:
"SMITH'S FALLS STORE BOTTLE"
Smith Falls, Ont.
Pint. **$35**

"SILVER SPRINGS DAIRY"Acton, Ont.
Pint. **$35**

"SUTTON DAIRY"
Sutton, Ont.
Pint. **$30**

Left to right:

"**CAMPBELL'S DAIRY PRODUCTS**" Peterborough, Ont. Pint. **$18**

"**LAITERIE LAURENTIAN DAIRY**" Pint. **$10**

"**JOHN DUNCAN**" 66 Drummond St., Montreal, Que. Pint. **$10**

"**YARMOUTH DAIRY**" Pint. **$10**

Left to right:

"**BEATON'S DAIRY PRODUCTS**"Oshawa, Ont. Pint. **$45**

"**RIODAN'S DAIRY**" Quart. **$65**

"**WHITBY DAIRY**"A.D. Soloway, 30 Palmerston Ave., Whitby, Ont. Pint. **$35**

"**THE GUARANTEED PURE MILK CO. LIMITED.**"Montreal, Que. Pint. **$15**

Left to right:
"STANDARD DAIRY"
Smith's Falls, Ont.
Pint. **$35**

"HURL'S DAIRY"Orillia, Ont.
Pint. **$35**

Left to right:
"BEATON'S DAIRY" Oshawa, Ont.
Pint. **$65**

"FEDERAL ICE CREAM"
Pint. **$30**

Left to right:
"WOODLAND DAIRY LTD." Parham.
Half-pint. **$20**

"OAKLAND DAIRY LTD."
Pint. **$20**

"COWAN'S LTD." Brockville, Ont.
Quart. **$20**

**"LAITERIE DES
PRODUCTEURS"**
**"Producer's Dairy
Inc."** Montreal, Que.
Quart. **$20**

"NORTHSIDE DAIRY"
Welland, Ont. Bottles of
this type, embossed with a
pattern, are scarce.
Half-pint. **$20**

Left to right:
FRUIT JUICE BOTTLE.
Quart. **$6**

**CHOCOLATE MILK
by Trufruit Wonder Drinks.**
7oz. **$10**

"BORDEN'S JUICE BOTTLE"
Quart. **$125**

**PROMOTIONAL
MINIATURES** Left to right:

"CITY DAIRY" Toronto.
$50

"BORDEN'S" $50

Left to right:
"BELLEVILLE CREAMERY LIMITED"
Half-pint. **$50**

"ELMHURST DAIRY LIMITED"
Montreal, Que.
Half-pint. **$15**

Left to right:
"ALLANDALE DAIRY"
Barrie, Ont.
Half-pint. **$35**

"SIMCOE SANITARY DAIRY"
Pint. **$15**

"FORT ERIE DAIRY CO."
Half-pint. **$15**

Left to Right:
"CEDAR DALE DAIRY"
Orono, Ont.
Half-pint. **$75**

"ELGIN DAIRIES"
St. Thomas, Ont.
Half-pint. **$15**

"IDEAL DAIRY"
Peterborough, Ont.
Half-pint. **$25**

Left to Right:
"RICHMOND HILL DAIRY"
Half-pint. **$35**

"CRESCENT DAIRY"
Half-pint. **$25**

"REID'S PASTEURIZED PRODUCTS" Belleville, Ont.
Half-pint. **$12**

QUARTER PINT CREAM BOTTLES
Above, left to right:

"Donlands Dairy" $35

"Dockeray's Dairy" $35

"Silver Crest Dairy" $35

"Findlay Dairy" $35

QUARTER PINT CREAM BOTTLES
Centre, left to right:
"Moore's Model Dairy"
Port Hope, Ont. $35

"Silverwood's Safe Milk" $35

Left to right:
"PURITY MILK PRODUCTS" Smith's Falls, Ont. Quarter-pint. $35
"COUNTRY SIDE DAIRY" Windsor & Comber, Ont. Quarter-pint. $35
"CITIZEN'S DAIRY" Belleville, Ont. Quarter-pint $25
"CLOVERDALE DAIRY LTD. Toronto, Ont. Quarter-pint. $35

Sour Cream Containers

Above, left to right:

"SILVERWOOD'S" Pint **$45**

"BIRD'S HILL DAIRY PRODUCTS" Toronto, Ont.
Half-pint. **$50**

"FRAN RESTAURANTS" Toronto, Ont.
12 oz. **$60**

Above:
"CAULFIELD'S" Toronto, Ont.
Pint. **$60**

NOTE:

Most Canadian dairy bottles and containers were made by the Consumers Glass Company Limited or the Dominion Glass Company Limited. Company trade marks are embossed on the base of bottles (Canadian glass manufacturer's trade marks are illustrated and listed in this book).

Bottles made in the United States are also marked by the manufacturer, one being the Thatcher Manufacturing Co. who made Laurentia Dairy bottles.

"GOLD STAR DAIRY"
Toronto, Ont.
$50

Milk Bottles with Applied Coloured Labels

Left:

"GIMBLETT'S DAIRY" Oshawa, Ont. Commemorating Coronation of George VI and Queen Elizabeth, 1937. Quart **$800**

Not Shown:

"NEWCASTLE DAIRY" R.E. LeGresley, Newcastle, Ont. Commemorating Coronation of George VI and Queen Elizabeth 1937. Pint **$600**

Right:

"R. CLARKE DAIRY LTD." Ottawa, Ont. Commemorating Royal Visit to Canada by King George and Queen Elizabeth, 1939. Quart **$450**

Not Shown:

"R. CLARKE DAIRY LTD." Ottawa, Ont. Commemorating Royal Visit to Canada by King George and Queen Elizabeth,Pint **$450**

Left to right: **Second World War Quarts.**

"PRINCE EDWARD DAIRIES" Picton, Ont. Churchill and V sign. **$500**

"GRACEFIELD DAIRY" "Like Our Air Force" **$450**

"HIGHCLERE DAIRY" Ottawa, Ont. Commemorating the meeting of President Roosevelt & Prime Minister Churchill at Quebec, 1944. **$800**

Left to right: **Second World War Bottles.**

"CLARKE DAIRY LTD." Ottawa, Ont. Quart **$400**

"CLARKE DAIRY LTD." Ottawa, Ont. Pint **$400**

"PORT HOPE CITY DAIRY" Quart **$300**

"DUNROBIN FARM DAIRY" Beaverton, Ont. Pint **$300**

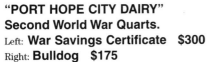

"PORT HOPE CITY DAIRY"
Second World War Quarts.
Left: **War Savings Certificate** **$300**
Right: **Bulldog** **$175**

"SUNSHINE DAIRY"
Peterborough, Ont.
World War II Bottle - servicemen
and slogan. Pint **$300**

"STUART'S DAIRY" Cobourg, Ont.
Half-pint **$75**

"THE HARRIS DAIRY"Shadow Hill
Farm Dairy Products. Gatineau, Que.
Pint **$50**

"HILL'S DAIRY" Meaford, Ont.
Quart **$125**

Left:
"HERRINGTON'S DAIRY"
Picton, Ont. Milkman and slogan.
Quart **$40**

Right:
"CENTRAL DAIRIES" Ottawa, Ont.
Quart **$75**

"KAWARTHA DAIRY"
Bobcaygeon, Ont.
Pint **$225**

"KAWARTHA DAIRY"
Bobcaygeon, Ont.
Baby carrying bottle
with slogan.
Quart **$200**

"COWAN'S DAIRY"
Brockville, Ont.
Quart **$75**
Not Shown:
"COWAN'S DAIRY"
Brockville, Ont.
Pint **$75**

**"THE PURE
MILK CO. LTD."**
Charlottetown, P.E.I.
Quart **$45**

"ALPHA DAIRY"
Calgary, Alberta
Pint **$25**

Left to right:

"**LONG SAULT DAIRY**" Pint $100

"**COMMUNITY DAIRY**" Kapuskasing, Ont. Quart $150

"**RUTHERFORD'S DAIRY**" Havelock, Ont. Quart $95

"**GLENLEA DAIRY**" (Ontario dairy) With rhyme. Quart $95

"**PRINCE EDWARD DAIRIES**"
Picton, Ont. Half-pint $30

"**CO-OP**" Saskatchewan Co-operative
Creamery Association Limited.
Pint $30

"CLARKE DAIRY" Ottawa, Ont.
Barbara Ann Scott with slogan.
Pint **$750 - 1,000**
Barbara Ann Scott, gold medal winner,
women's singles figure skating, 1948
winter Olympics.

"LEE GRILL'S DAIRY" Belleville, Ont.
Marilyn Bell with slogan.
Pint **$65**
Sixteen year old Marilyn Bell,
the first person to swim Lake Ontario,
September 9, 1954.

Left:
"CITIZEN'S DAIRY" Belleville, Ont.
Baseball and hockey player with slo-
gan. Half-pint **$50**
Right:
"JOHNSTONE DAIRIES LIMITED"
Moose Jaw, Sask. On reverse,
baseball and hockey player with
slogan. Pint **$25**

"MEADOWBROOK DAIRY"
Murphy Bros., Bobcaygeon, Ont.
Fishermen with slogan.
Pint **$250**

Left to right:

"SIMCOE SANITARY DAIRY" Quart   **$20**

"OAKVILLE DAIRY" Quart   **$10**

"MAPLE LEAF DAIRY" Quart   **$20**

Left to right:

"CO-OP" Calgary, Alberta. Quart   **$20**

"HOLMES DAIRY" Napanee, Ont. Quart   **$15**

ALUMINUM POURING CASE.

Converts square quart into pitcher.   **$18**

"ROSEBAY DAIRY"
Napanee, Ont. Football player with slogan. Half-pint   **$30**

Above left:
"MASON DAIRY"
St. Catharines, Ont.
Lacrosse player with slogan.
Half-pint   **$95**

Above right:
"WOODWARD'S DAIRY"
St. Catharines, Ont.
Baseball player with slogan.
Half-pint.   **$95**

Left:
"HOOVER'S DAIRY"
Port Rowan, Ont. Quart   **$125**

Right:
"CENTRAL DAIRIES LTD."
Ottawa, Ont. Quart   **$75**

Left to right:
"EL CARMEN FARMS LTD."
Pint   **$50**

"ROBB'S DAIRY"
London, Ont. Pint   **$95**

"CLOVERHILL DAIRY"
Gore Bay, Ont. Pint   **$75**

Left to Right:

"**SUNSHINE DAIRY CO. LTD.**" St. John's Nfld.
On reverse, baby with milk bottle. Quart **$50**

"**MOHAN-HUNTER DAIRY LIMITED**" Peterborough, Ont. Quart **$75**

"**CAMPBELL'S DAIRY PRODUCTS**" Peterborough, Ont. Quart **$125**

Left to Right:

"**CAMPBELL'S DAIRY PRODUCTS**" Peterborough, Ont. Pint **$125**

"**KRIM-KO**" (A franchise name used by a number of dairies). Half-pint **$45**

"**PALM DAIRIES LTD.**" (Western Canada Dairy) Half-pint. **$95**

Left to Right:

"CLANCEY'S DAIRY"
Quart **$195**

"MILLIGAN'S DAIRY"
Napanee, Ont.
Quart **$95**

"IRVING'S DAIRY"
Norwood, Ont.
Quart **$95**

Left to Right:

"HUTTON'S DAIRY"
Lindsay, Ont.
Quart **$150**

"GLENWOOD FARMS"
Lakefield, Ont.
Quart **$200**

"KAWARTHA DAIRY"
Bobcaygeon, Ont.
Quart **$150**

Left to Right:

"JORDAN'S DAIRY"
Kentville, N.S.
Quart **$50**

"IDEAL DAIRY"
Oshawa, Ont.
Quart **$200**

"LAITERIE ALFRED"
Montreal, Que.
Quart **$40**

Left to Right:
"BROOKFIELD'S ICE CREAM LTD."
Cornerbrook, Nfld.
Quart **$50**

"CO-OP DAIRY LTD."
Newcastle, N.B.
Quart **$35**

"KELOWNA CREAMERY LTD."
Quart **$50**

Left:
"PORT HOPE CITY DAIRY"
Quart **$75**

Right:
"PORT HOPE CITY DAIRY"
Quart **$75**

Left to Right:
"WALKERTON DAIRY"
Quart **$65**

"HOOPER'S DAIRY PRODUCTS"
Quart **$75**

"IDEAL DAIRY"
Hanover, Ont.
Quart **$75**

Left to right:

"BUTLER'S DAIRY" Belleville, Ont.
Pint **$50**

"POLLARD'S DAIRY"
Pint **$50**

"SCOTT'S DAIRY" Tillsonburg, Ont.
Pint **$50**

Left to right:

"THUNDER BAY DAIRY"
Pint **$50**

"COBOURG CITY DAIRY"
Pint **$65**

"WEST FLAMBORO DAIRY"
Pint **$75**

Left to right:

"RIVERVIEW DAIRY"
Caledonia, Ont. Pint **$50**

"HERRINGTON'S DAIRY"
Picton, Ont. Pint **$50**

Left to Right:

"LAKESIDE DAIRY"
Burlington, Ont. Half-pint **$65**

"W.L. RALPH'S DAIRY"
Brockville, Ont. Quarter-pint **$75**

"MONCRIEF'S DAIRY"
Peterborough, Ont. Half-pint **$200**

"WHITFIELD-MORRISON DAIRY" Peterborough, Ont.
Pint **$250**

Not Shown: **DAIRY BOTTLES WITH APPLIED COLOURED LABELS**

"BEATON'S DAIRY"
Oshawa, Ont. Quart **$95**

"CALNAN'S DAIRY"
Picton, Ont. On reverse, milkman and slogan.
Quart **$25**

Left to Right:

"SUNSHINE DAIRY CO." St. John's Nfld.
Half-pint **$50**

"HILLS QUALITY DAIRY PRODUCTS"
Saskatoon, Sask. Half-pint **$50**

"MODEL DAIRIES"
Calgary, Alberta Half-pint **$50**

Not Shown: **DAIRY BOTTLES WITH APPLIED COLOURED LABELS**

"FOSTER'S DAIRY"
Tweed, Ont. On reverse, lady drinking glass of milk and slogan. Half-pint **$75**

"McMULLEN'S DAIRY"
Lindsay, Ont. Half-pint **$150**

"NEWCASTLE DAIRY"
On reverse, building and slogan.
Pint **$125**

"PORT PERRY DAIRY"
On reverse, baby with milk bottle over his shoulder and slogan.
Quart **$300**

"WRIGHT'S DAIRY"
Cambellford, Ont. On reverse, sandwiches and glass of milk with slogan.
Half-pint **$125**

Left to Right:

"CEDARHILL DAIRY" Galt, Ont.
Half-pint **$95**

"LAKEVIEW DAIRY" Cobourg, Ont.
Half-pint **$75**

"RUTHERFORD'S DAIRY"
Havelock, Ont. Half-pint **$95**

"LINDSAY CREAMERY LIMITED"
Quarter-pint **$75**; half-pint **$85**; pint **$125** and quart **$125.**

Left to Right: **Quarter pint cream bottles.**

"ST. MARY'S STORE BOTTLE"	**$40**
"WILSON'S" Trenton, Ont.	**$40**
"BAXTER'S DAIRY" Goderich, Ont.	**$75**
"CHAPLIN'S DAIRY" Perth, Ont.	**$75**

Milk Bottles not Illustrated Applied Coloured Labels

A labeling process developed in the United States during the 1920's which came into popular use during the '30's on milk and soft drink bottles.

A paste made of borasilicate, oil and a colouring oxide was applied to bottles through a steel screen. The labeled bottle then had to be baked at a temperature of about 300 degrees Fahrenheit. If the label consisted of two colours the first colour applied had to dry before the next one could be added. A slow and expensive process.

In the 1940's it was discovered that by using a plastic resin in place of the oil in the mixture, drying time between applications of colour was almost eliminated, thus speeding the process and making it a more common procedure.

ANDREW DAIRY Goderich, Ont.
Square quart **$28**

AVON DAIRIES Stratford, Ont.
Reverse "V for Victory."
Round half-pint **$195**

BARTRAM'S DAIRY Ingersoll,
Ont. On reverse illustration of a baby. Round pint **$95**

BATESON'S MODEL DAIRY Wingham, Ont. Square quart **$15**

BEAMSVILLE DAIRY
Square quart **$20**

BROOKFIELD'S ICE CREAM LTD. Cornerbrook, Newfoundland.
Round quart **$50**

BUTLER'S DAIRY Belleville, Ont.
Round pint **$40**

CALNAN'S DAIRY, Picton.
Quart **$25**

CEDAR HILL DAIRY, Galt.
Square quart **$28**

CEDAR HILL DAIRY, Galt.
Round half-pint **$75**

CHRISTIE'S DAIRY.
Square quart **$18**

COBOURG CITY DAIRY.
Round Pint **$75**

CO-OP DAIRY LTD., Newcastle, New Brunswick.
Square quart **$35**

CRACKERTON'S DAIRY, New Hamburg.
Square quart. **$25**

CRYSTAL DAIRY, Harriston.
Square quart **$25**

DURHAM DAIRY, Listowel.
Round quart **$45**

EVENHOLME DAIRY, Elmira.
Round pint **$65**

FAIRFIELD MODERN DAIRY, Hamilton.
Square quart **$25**

FINNEGAN'S DAIRY, Stratford.
Square quart **$20**

FOREMOST DAIRIES, Kitchener & Stratford.
Round half-pint **$65**

GLOVER'S CITY DAIRY, Chatham.
Square quart **$15**

GLOVER'S CITY DAIRY, Chatham.
Round half-pint **$65**

GLOVER'S JAS., DAIRY, Alymer.
Round quart **$65**

HEARN'S DAIRY, St. Mary's.
Square quart **$15**

HERRINGTON'S DAIRY, Picton.
Round pint **$65**

HILLCREST DAIRY, Hamilton.
Square quart **$25**

HILL'S QUALITY DAIRY,
Saskatoon, Saskatchewan.
Round half-pint **$50**

HOLMES DAIRY, Napanee.
Square quart **$15**

JERSEY DAIRY, Wallaceburg.
Square quart **$20**

KENNEDY'S SANITARY DAIRY,
Leamington.
Square pint **$45**

KENT DAIRY, Chatham.
Round pint **$65**

LAKE DRIVE DAIRY, Bracebridge.
Square quart **$30**

LAMBTON-KENT CREAMERIES,
Wallaceburg.
Square pint **$26**

MACNICOLL'S DAIRY, Brantford.
Slogan on reverse.
Round pint **$65**

MAPLE LEAF DAIRY, Preston.
Square pint **$40**

MAPLE LEAF DAIRY, Seaforth.
Square quart **$28**

MILROY DAIRY, Stratford.
Square quart **$18**

MILROY DAIRY, Stratford.
Square half-pint **$35**

MITCHELL CREAMERY, Mitchell.
Round half-pint **$95**

OAKVILLE DAIRY.
Square quart **$10**

OAKVILLE DAIRY.
Round half-pint **$95**

PALMERSTON DAIRY.
Round half-pint **$80**

PARKER'S DAIRY. Norwich.
Square quart **$25**

PRESTON DAIRY.
Square quart **$32**

PURITY DAIRY, Listowel.
Round quart. **$45**

PURITY PRODUCTS LIMITED,
Brantford.
Round quart **$95**

RIDEALGH DAIRY, Sarnia.
Square pint **$30**

RIDGE DAIRY, Ridgeway.
Square quart **$25**

RIVERVIEW DAIRY, Caledonia.
On reverse Baseball player.
Round half-pint **$65**

SCOTT'S DAIRY, Tillsonburg.
Square pint **$35**

SCOTT'S DAIRY, Tillsonburg.
Round half-pint **$50**

SPRING VALLEY FARM, Paris.
Square quart **$20**

STACEY BROS. LTD., Mitchell.
Round half-pint **$65**

SUNNYBROOK DAIRY, Watertown.
Square quart **$18**

SUNSHINE DAIRY CO. LTD.
St. John's Newfoundland.
Round quart **$50**

SUNSHINE DAIRY CO. LTD.
St. John's Newfoundland.
Round 1/2 pint **$50**

TERRACE HILL DAIRY, Brantford.
Square quart **$25**

TERRACE HILL DAIRY, Brantford.
Round half-pint **$95**

THUNDER BAY DAIRY.
Round pint **$50**

VALLEY CITY DAIRY, Dundas.
Square quart **$18**

WALKERTON DAIRIES.
Square quart **$26**

WALKERTON DAIRY,
Round quart **$75**
WILLOW GROVE CREAMERY,
Mitchell. Round pint **$95**

WILLOW GROVE CREAMERY,
Mitchell. Round half-pint **$75**

Individual Creamers

CREAMERS $30 Each
Borden's; Eplett; Homecrest Dairy and Ideal Dairy: 3/4 ounce.
Sealtest: 1/2 ounce.

Left to Right:

"WILSON'S"	$30
"BENWARE CREAMERY"	$30
"DAIRYLEA"	$30

Left to Right:

"ROSEBUD CREAMERY"	$30
"CENTRAL DAIRIES LTD."	$30
"MIDWEST"	$30

Dairy "Go-Withs"

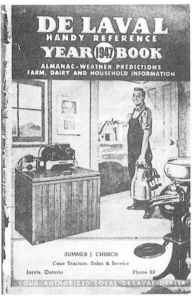

Many types of "Go-Withs" related to the dairy industry can be found, some examples are illustrated in this section. Items from the farm or dairy, such as milk cans, cow bells, cream separators or bowls and churns etc., used for butter and cheese making, along with calendars, advertisements, bottle cases or carriers would be interesting additions to a dairy bottle collection

DE LAVAL YEAR BOOK. 1947.
48 Pages. In good condition.
$30

COW & CALF Litho tin advertisements for De Laval
Cream Separators. 1920 - 30. **Each $45**

Advertising copy on back of cow: "De Laval Cream Separators save $10 to $15 per cow every year. World's standard, over 2,325,000 in daily use. The De Laval Separator Co., New York, Chicago, San Francisco, Winnipeg, Montreal, Peterboro, Vancouver. Local agents everywhere."

Cardboard Dairy Containers

Many items relating to dairies, including waxed cartons are being sought by collectors.

Back row, left to right: **$5** **$20** **$20** **$8**
Front row left to right: **$ 4** **$8** **$4**

$10 each

$10 each

Left to Right:
THERMOMETER. "Hemlock Park Dairy, Kingston, Ont." Ht. 8 1/2" **$30**
MILKSHAKE CONTAINER. "Hemlock Park Dairy, Kingston, Ont." **$10**
MILKSHAKE CONTAINER $8

"BORDEN'S DELIVERY TRUCK" By Buddy-L. 1950's-60's.
Plexiglass windshield and windows, composition tires.
One door missing. L. 11" **$65**

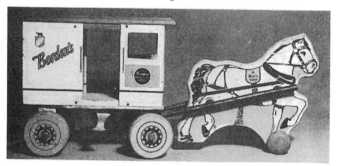

"BORDEN'S" HORSE DRAWN WAGON.
1930's Wood. L. 20" **$400**

Dairy Bottle Caps

Milk bottle caps make an attractive and easily displayed collectable for anyone interested in items related to dairy bottles. The selection illustrated is a sample of the type of cap which might be collected from most areas in Canada.

The large caps are 1 3/4" in diameter. The mid-size (1 1/4" diam.) is from a later type of bottle. The smallest (1" diam.) is restaurant creamer size.

At this time most caps may be bought from between **$1.00** and **$4.00**.

Dairy Tokens

Made of brass and plain or coloured aluminum the purpose of the dairy token was to replace cash which was easily stolen from bottles left outside the door. They also served the purpose of making an order without writing it as they came with the quantity and type of product required. The first tokens were round and dropped into the bottle. This caused a problem since they froze and could not be removed easily. Later ones were made in shapes that would rest in the neck of the bottle. All types of dairy tokens make an interesting and easily displayed dairy collectable.

Values range from **$2.00** to **$20.00**.

Fruit Jars

Fruit jars have been manufactured in Canada since 1865 and many varieties were made at several glass factories across the country. Each type is classified by a name or symbol embossed on the jar.

The method used to manufacture fruit jars helps in dating them. Canadian jars, hand blown in the mold, with a ground lip date from 1865: 1906. Semi-automatic and automatic machines were used to produce jars after 1906, jars made in this manner have a smooth lip, an improvement for effective sealing.

The most common type of closure found on Canadian fruit jars is the metal screw band which hold a glass lid and rubber ring in place. Early jars had cork stoppers which were sealed with wax, but because this was not a reliable method of sealing refinements were made and a glass lid held in place with an iron clamp was introduced. Jars with this type of closure were made for two or three years (1865 – 1867) at the Hamilton Glass Works, Hamilton, Ontario.

Sealers with the adjustable "Lightning Seal" were made in Canada from about 1910 – 1920. However, after being used several times the wires that held the glass lid in place would become loose and a tight seal could not be achieved.

Collectors are interested in fruit jars with variations in the embossed lettering. On some jars styles are mixed, on others letters are backwards, also molds with words mis-spelled were used in the production of some jars.

Sealers were sold by some firms as packers or product jars containing coffee, corn syrup and pickles etc. Jars of this type with the original paper label intact are an interesting addition to a collection.

Fruit jars can be found in shades of "bottle green" (aqua, bluish-green, greenish-blue etc.) as well as amber, blue, clear and suncast. Amber jars generally bring premium prices.

Canadian jars were made in American and Imperial measure. The sizes and their equivalent in ounces are as follows:

AMERICAN (Am.)
1/2 Pint – 8 oz.
Pint – 16 oz
Quart – 32 oz.
1/2 Gallon – 64 oz.

IMPERIAL (Imp.)
1/2 Pint – 10 oz.
Pint – 20 oz.
Quart – 40 oz.
1/2 Gallon – 80 oz.

"ACME LG CO. TRADEMARK 1893" Reverse "Mason's patent Nov. 30, 1858"

"ACME" (Ground Lip)
Factory: Lamont Glass Company
Am. Pint   **$200 - $300**
Am. Quart   **$100 - $200**
Am. Half-Gallon   **$200 - $300**

"ACME SEAL" (Smooth Lip)
Factory: Manitoba Glass
Manufacturing Company.
Am. Pint   **$140**
Am. Quart   **$55**
Am. Half-Gallon   **$55**

"THE AMERICAN PORCELAIN LINED" (Ground Lip)
Factory: North American Glass Co.
Am. Pint   **$225**
Am. Quart   **$30**
Am. Half-Gallon   **$25**

Original "Boyd" cap with mono-gram "NAGCo" embossed on zinc cap and milk glass liner.   **$20**

Note: All metal lids especially zinc, imparted a metallic taste to the contents of a jar and was one of the failings of the early Mason lid. The Boyd cap, patented in 1869, solved this problem by using a milk glass lid combined with a zinc screw cap.

"ANCHOR" - Slanted. (Smooth Lip)
Factory: Possibly Sydenham
Glass Company.
Am. Pint **$300 - $500**
Am. Quart **$50 - $100**
Am. Half-Gallon **$50 - $100**

"ANCHOR" - Small Straight.
(Smooth Lip)
Factory: Possibly Sydenham
Glass Company.
Am. Quart **$400 - $600**

"ANCHOR" - Large Straight.
(Smooth Lip)
Factory: Possibly Sydenham
Glass Company.
Am. Quart **$400 - $600**

"BEAVER" (Ground Lip)

Factories: The Ontario Glass Works; The Sydenham Glass Company. Beaver fruit jars were made in both American and Imperial measure, usually the Imperial type are marked "I M P" on base.

Beaver facing right - Clear
Pint   **$80**
Quart   **$25**
Half-Gallon   **$45**

Beaver facing right - Sediment amber
Pint   **$800**
Quart   **$600**
Half-Gallon   **$600**

Beaver facing right - True amber
Pint   **$1000**
Quart   **$650**

Beaver facing left - Clear
Pint   **$300**
Quart   **$300**
Half-Gallon   **$300**

Beaver facing left - True amber
Pint   **$1,500**
Quart   **Price unknown**

"BEEHIVE" (Smooth Lip)
Factory: Dominion Glass Company
Am. Pint **$500**
Am. Quart **$150**
Am. Half-Gallon **$150**
Note: Robert Simpson Co. Ltd., Toronto registered the Beehive trademark to be used on fruit jars March 10, 1902.

"BEST (Ground Lip & Smooth Lip)
Factories: Diamond Glass Co. Ltd.;
Diamond Flint Glass Co. Ltd.;
Dominion Glass Company.
Am. Quart **$30**
Am. Half-Gallon **$35**
Am. Quart or Half-Gallon
in amber **$350**

"BLUE RIBBON COFFEE" (Smooth Lip)
Factory: Dominion Glass Company.
Am. Quart with label and
original top **$15**
Am. Quart without label **$5**

"THE BURLINGTON" (Ground Lip)
Factory: Burlington Glass Works.
Am. Quart **$60**
Am. Half-Gallon **60**
Am. Quart with
mold maker's error **$60**

"CANADA N E S W" (Ground Lip)
Factory: Attributed to the Lamont
Glass Company.
Am. Pint **$385**
Am. Quart **$225**
Am. Half-Gallon **$225**
*When found in yellow amber price
would be $1,500 and up.*

"CANADIAN KING" (Smooth Lip)
Factory: Consumers Glass Company.
Am. Pint **$40**
Am. Quart **$25**
Am. Half-Gallon **$50 - $100**

"CANADIAN QUEEN" (Smooth
Lip)
Factory: Consumers Glass
Company.
Am. Quart **$250**

"CARROLL'S TRUE SEAL" (Smooth
Lip)
Factory: Unknown, made for a chain
of stores in the London and
Hamilton, Ontario area.
Am. Pint **$50 - $100**
Am. Quart **$50 - $100**
Am. Half-Gallon **$50 - $100**

"COLUMBIA" (Smooth Lip)
Factory: Unknown
Am. Pint   **$200 - 300**
Am. Quart   **$150 - $250**

"CORONA JAR" (Smooth Lip)
Factory" Consumers Glass Company.
Am. Pint, Quart and Half-Gallon   **$2 - $3**

"IMPROVED CORONA" (Smooth Lip)
Factory: Consumers Glass Company.
Am. Pint, Quart and Half-Gallon   **$2 - $3**

"CORONET" (Smooth Lip)
Factory: Crystal Glass Company.
Am. Pint embossed "Coronet"
with Crown emblem   **$150**

Am. Quart embossed "Coronet"
with Coronet emblem   **$150**

Am. Half-Gallon embossed
"Coronet" with Coronet emblem   **$150**

"CROWN" fruit jar were made by several Canadian factories and more than 60 variations of this type of jar have been identified. The "No-Dot Crown" is considered to be the earliest and has a simple crown emblem. Later jars had a variety of crowns embossed, some of them quite ornate and often with only minor differences. In the case of the "Heart-Shaped Crown" there are six variations of the emblem.

Often considerable study is necessary to find the subtle differences and it would be quite an accomplishment to gather a collection with every variation.

"CROWN" - Eaton's embossed on reverse "The T. Eaton Co. Limited, 190 Yonge St., Toronto, Can."
(Smooth Lip)
Factory: Dominion Glass Company.
Am. Pint **$100 - $200**
Am. Quart **$50 - $100**
Am. Half-Gallon **$50 - $100**

"CROWN" - Eaton's embossed on reverse "E" in a diamond and "Toronto & Winnipeg."
(Smooth Lip)
Factory: Dominion Glass Company.
Am. Pint **$15**
Am. Quart **$10**
Am. Half-Gallon **$20**

"CROWN" - Bulge
(Ground Lip & Smooth Lip)
Factories: North American Glass Co.; Diamond Glass Co. Ltd.; Diamond Flint Glass Co. Ltd.
Am. Quart **$15**
Am. Half-Gallon **$12**
Imp. Pint **$40**

"CROWN" - Heart Shaped
(Ground Lip)
Factory: Burlington Glass Works.
Am. Quart **$10 - $15**
Am. Half-Gallon **$10 - $15**
Imp. Pint **$30 - $40**
Imp. Quart **$10 - $15**
Imp. Half-Gallon **$10 - $15**

"CROWN" - Heart Shaped, no
word. (Ground Lip)
Factory: Burlington Glass Works.
Imp. Quart **$100 - $200**

"CROWN" - Hybrid (Ground Lip)
Factory: Unknown
Am. Quart with good embossing
$50 - $100

"CROWN" - No Dot (Ground Lip)
Factory: Hamilton Glass Works
Am. Pint **$500 - $700**
Am. Quart **$15**
Am. Half-Gallon **$15**

"**CROWN**" - Ring (Ground Lip)
Factory: North American Glass Co.
Am. Quart **$15**
Am. Half-Gallon **$15**
Am. Quart with
Crown emblem only **$30**

"**CROWN**" - Tall Narrow
(Ground Lip)
Factory: Attributed to the Hamilton
Glass Works.
Am. Pint **$45**

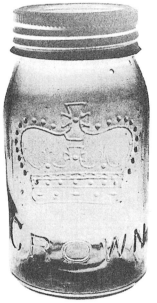

"**CROWN**"
Apple Green (Smooth Lip)
Factory: Dominion Glass Company.
Am. Quart **$25**

"**CROWN**" - Improved (Smooth Lip)
Factory: Dominion Glass Company.
Am. Pint **$1**
Am. Quart **$1**
Am. Half-Gallon **$1**
Am. Quart with cross embossed
on reverse **$50**

"D G CO" (Ground Lip)
Factory: Diamond Glass Co. Ltd.
Am. Quart   **$45**
Am. Half-Gallon   **$45**

"THE DARLING" (Ground Lip)
Factory: Hamilton Glass Works
Am. Pint   **$250**
Am. Quart   **$35**
Am. Half-Gallon   **$35**
Imp. Pint   **$250**
Imp. Quart   **$35**
Imp. Half-Gallon   **$45**

"DIAMOND" (Smooth Lip)
Factory: Dominion Glass Company
Am. Pint   **$40**
Am. Quart   **$25**
Am. Half-Gallon   **$30**
Am. Pint - Aqua   **$60**

"THE DIAMOND NOVA SCOTIA"
(Ground Lip)
Factory: The Humphreys Glass Co.
or The Lamont Glass Co.
Am. Pint   **$850**
Am. Quart   **$225**
Am. Half-Gallon   **$225**

"DOMINION (Ground Lip)
Factory: The (Early) Dominion
Glass Company
Am. Pint   **$250 - $500**
Am. Quart   **$100 - $200**
Am. Half-Gallon   **$150 - $250**

"DOMINION WIDE MOUTH
 - Made in The British Empire"
(Smooth Lip)
Factory: Unknown.
Am. Pint   **$35**
Am. Quart   **$30**

"DOMINION WIDE MOUTH SPECIAL" (Smooth Lip)
Factory: Dominion Glass Company
Am. Pint   **$6**
Am. Quart   **$2**
Am. Half-Gallon   **$3**

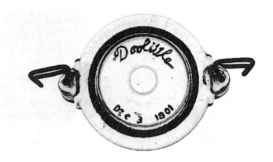

"DOOLITTLE" (Smooth Lip)

Factory: Sydenham Glass Company

Plain jars with an unusual closure, the glass lid has two metal ears that swing round and hook over the neck. The lids are embossed "Doolittle, patented Dec. 3, 1901" and "Doolittle, patented Jan. 2 & June 12, 1900 – match cover and slots."

Am. Pint   **$90**
Am. Quart   **$30**
Am. Half-Gallon   **$35**
Imp. Half-Pint (Square)   **$150**
Imp. Pint (Square)   **$150**
Imp. Half-Pint (Jelly Jar)   **$100**
Imp. Pint (Jelly Jar)   **$100**

"DYSON'S (Smooth Lip)
Factory: Dominion Glass Company.
Dyson's, producers of pickles and extracts etc., sold some of their products in this type of jar.
Am. Quart **$22**

"EDWARDSBURG CORN SYRUP"
(Smooth Lip)
Factory: Dominion Glass Company.
Quart perfect seal jar **$50**

"EMPRESS" (Ground Lip)
Factory: Unknown
Am. Quart **$400 - $600**

"ERIE FRUIT JAR" (Ground Lip)
Factory: Erie Glass Company.
Am. Pint **$500**
Am. Quart **$110**
Am. Half-Gallon **$115**
Imp. Pint **$355**
Imp. Quart **$135**
Imp. Half-Gallon **$195**
Quart (amber) with only
"ERIE" on base **$200**

"ERIE FRUIT JAR" On reverse
"T. Eaton Co. Limited, Toronto"
On base "Erie." (Ground Lip)
Factory: Erie Glass Company
Am. Pint **$600**
Am. Quart **$500+**

"ERIE LIGHTNING" (Smooth Lip)
Factory: Dominion Glass Company
Am. Quart **$100**

"FEARMAN'S MINCE MEAT -
Hamilton" (Smooth Lip)
Factory: Unknown
Am. Quart **$40**

"GEM: RUTHERFORD & CO."
(Ground Lip)
Factories: Hamilton Glass Works;
Burlington Glass Works.
Am. Pint **$1,500**
Am. Quart **$20**
Am. Half-Gallon **$30**

"THE GEM" (Ground Lip)
Factory: Hamilton Glass Works.
Am. Pint **$18**
Am. Quart **$5**
Am. Half-Gallon **$5**

"GEM" - With Hero Cross.
(Ground Lip)
Factory: The Burlington Glass Works
bought the rights to produce this jar
in Canada.
Am. Pint **$60**
Am. Quart **$10**
Am. Half-Gallon **$10**

"GEM" - Nova Scotia Arched.
(Ground Lip)
Factory: The Humphreys Glass Co.,
The Lamont Glass Co., or the Nova
Scotia Glass Co.
Am. Quart - **Rare, too few known
to price.**

"GEM: Wallaceburg" (Smooth Lip)
Factory: Sydenham Glass Company.
Am. Pint **$10**
Am. Quart **$3**
Am. Half-Gallon **$4**
Imp. Pint **$10**
Imp. Quart **$2**
Imp. Half-Gallon **$3**

"IMPROVED GEM" (Smooth Lip)
Factories: Diamond Flint Glass Co.;
Dominion Glass Company.
Am. Pint **$8**
Am. Quart **$5**
Am. Half-Gallon **$5**

"GREEK KEY" (Safety Valve)
(Ground Lip)
Factory: Hamilton Glass Works.
Am. Quart (complete) **$85**
Am. Half-Gallon (complete) **$85**

"GREEK KEY" (Tin Top)
(Ground Lip)
Factory: Burlington Glass Works.
Am. Quart **$100**
Am. Half-Gallon **$70**

"HAMILTON GLASS WORKS" (Applied Lip)

Factory: Hamilton Glass Works.

Embossed "Hamilton Glass Works 1 Quart" glass lid with iron clamp. **$200**

Embossed "Hamilton Glass Works 1 Quart" corker. **$250**

Embossed with mold maker's error – "Hamilton Glass Works 'Olamp' Jar 1/2 Gal" **$150 - $300**

No. 1: Corker. Am. Pint **$1,000 - $2,000**

No. 2 Clamp. Am. Quart **$400**

No. 3 Clamp. Am. Half-Gallon **$250 - $500**

No. 4 Corker. Am. Gallon **$800 - $1,200**

No. 4 Clamp. Am. Gallon **$800 - $1,200**

COMPARISON OF CLAMP & CORKER MOUTH. Clamp jar on left has recess to hold wax.

"HAMILTON GLASS WORKS" Left to Right

No. 1 Clamp jar, glass lid with iron clamp. Am. Pint **$1,000 - $2,000**

No. 2 Corker. Am. Quart **$500**

No. 3 Corker. Am. Half-Gallon **$500**

"THE IDEAL" (Ground Lip)
Factory: Foster Brothers Glass
Works, Port Colborne, Ontario.
Am. Pint **$30**
Am. Quart **$8**
Am. Half-Gallon **$10**
Glass lid embossed "The Ideal" **$30**

"THE IDEAL IMPERIAL QT."
(Ground Lip)
Factory: Foster Brothers Glass
Works, Port Colborne, Ontario.
Imp. Pint **$210**
Imp. Quart **$27**
Imp. Half-Gallon **$80**

"THE IMPERIAL" - With monogram
"E G Co" (Ground Lip)
Factory: Excelsior Glass Company.

With good embossing:
Imp. Pint **$30**
Imp. Quart **$10**
Imp. Half-Gallon **$30**

With poor embossing:
Imp. Pint **$20**
Imp. Quart **$4**
Imp. Half-Gallon **$6**

Lids with good embossing:
"Excelsior Glass Co. Incorporated 1879"
or "Excelsior Glass Co., Register'd
Apr. 19. 79" **$35**

"IMPROVED JAM" (Ground Lip)
Factory: Lamont Glass Company.
Embossed monogram on reverse:
"L G Co"
Am. Pint **$300**
Am. Quart **$150**
Am. Half-Gallon **$150**

"JEWEL JAR"
(Smooth Lip)
Factory: Consumers
Glass Company.
Am. Pint **$5**
Am. Quart **$3**
Am. Half-Gallon **$3**

"CANADIAN JEWEL"
(Smooth Lip)
Factory: Consumers Glass Company.
Am. Pint, Quart
and Half-Gallon **$2 - $3**

"IMPROVED JEWEL"
(Smooth Lip)
Factory: Consumers Glass
Company.
Am. Pint **$7**
Am. Quart **$4**
Am. Half-Gallon **$8**

"JEWEL JAR"- Stippled Shield
(Smooth Lip)
Factory: Consumers Glass Company.
Am. Half-Gallon **$65**

"JEWEL JAR" - Plain Shield
(Smooth Lip)
Factory: Consumers Glass Company.
Am. Pint **$9**
Am. Quart **$7**
Am. Half-Gallon **$10**

"KING" (Smooth Lip)
A Smalley, Kivlan and Onthank
design possibly made in Canada by
Consumers Glass Company.
Am. Half-Pint **$45**
Am. Pint **$25**
Am. Quart **$17**
Am. Half-Gallon **$38**

"MASON FRUIT JAR"
(Smooth Lip)
Factory: Made in Canada by
Dominion Glass Company.
Am. Pint **$5**
Am. Quart **$4**
(Illus. left) Jars with
reversed "N" **$45**

(Illus. right) Jars with mold
maker's error 'CANANA' **$40**

Any size "Mason Fruit Jar"
in amber **$135**

*Note: The original Mason Jar was patented in 1858 by John L. Mason of New York.
Still being manufactured to this day this type of jar was made in several variations in
factories in the United States and Canada.*

"MID WEST" (Smooth Lip)
Factory: Mid-West Glass Co.
Am. Pint **$8**
Am. Quart **$6**
Am. Half-Gallon **$5**

"NABOB BRAND" (Smooth Lip)
Factories: Consumers Glass Co.;
Dominion Glass Co.
Am. Quart, Round **$5**
  With original lid **$12**
Am. Quart, Square **$5**
  With original lid **$12**
Am. Quart, Oval **$9**

"PANSY"
Factory: Possibly Diamond Glass Co. Ltd.
Or the Diamond Flint Glass Co. Ltd.
On some "Pansy" jars the letters "B E S T"
can be seen faintly behind the name "Pansy."
The glass is fragile and the lips of these
jars are easily chipped, jars in mint
condition are scarce.
Am. Quart (mint) **$225**
Am. Quart (chipped lip) **$55**
Am. Half-Gallon (mint) **$225**
Am. Half-Gallon (chipped lip) **$55**
Amber jar (mint) **$525**
Amber jars (chipped lip) **$250**

"THE PERFECT SEAL" (Smooth Lip)
Factory: Dominion Glass Co.
Am. Pint **$5**
Am. Quart **$2**
Am. Half-Gallon **$2**

"PERFECT SEAL" (Smooth Lip)
Factory: Dominion Glass Co.
Am. Pint **$4**
Am. Quart **$2**
Am. Half-Gallon **$2**

"THE PERFECT SEAL"
(Smooth Lip)
Factory: Dominion Glass Co.
Am. Pint **$7**
Am. Quart **$2**
Am. Half-Gallon **$2**
Jars with mold maker's error:
"PERFECT" **$25**

"PERFECT SEAL" (Smooth Lip)
Factory: Dominion Glass Co.
Am. Pint **$3**
Am. Quart **$2**
Am. Half-Gallon **$2**

"PRINCESS" (Smooth Lip)
A Smalley, Kivlan and Onthank
design possibly produced in
Canada by Consumers Glass Co.
Am. Pint **$50 - $75**
Am. Quart **$50 - $75**

"Kant Krack" lid used on Smalley,
Kivlan & Onthank Queen jars.

"QUEEN"
"Improved Made in Canada" (Smooth Lip)
Factory: Consumers Glass Company.
Am. Pint **$10**
Am. Quart **$10**
Am. Half-Gallon **$10**
"Queen" with mold maker's error –
'Wide Muoth' (Illus.)
Am. Pint **$55**

The Queen jar was originally made in the United States from a design
by Smalley, Kivlan & Onthank whose patent for this jar was issued
Feb. 9, 1908, the maker of these jars is unknown. In the 1920's Consumers
Glass Company of Toronto was licensed to produce Queen jars in Canada.

Queen jars made by the Consumers Glass Company are embossed
"Improved Made in Canada" round the neck. The "Kant Krack" lid, secured
by side clips is used on these jars.

"ROGERS GOLDEN SYRUP"
(Smooth Lip)
Factory: Dominion Glass Co.
Am. Quart **$75 - $125**

"THE ROSE" (Smooth Lip)
Factory: Unknown, possibly the
Sydenham Glass Company.
Am. Pint **$150 - $250**
Am. Quart **$28**
Am. Half-Gallon **$28**
Imp. Pint embossed "IMP" on base
$250 - $350

"SAFETY SEAL" (Smooth Lip)
Factory: Consumers Glass Co.
Am. Pint **$10**
Am. Quart **$8**
Am Half-Gallon **$8**

Not Shown:
**"SCHRAM AUTOMATIC SEALER
B Trade Mark Registered"**
(Smooth Lip)
Factory: Dominion Glass Co.
Imp. Pint **$6**
Imp. Quart **$4**
Imp. Half-Gallon **$4**
Canadian lids with good gasket
$25 - $35
These one piece metal lids are
found marked as follows:
"Schram Bottle Cap, Patd 1901
& 3, Woodstock, Ont. Canada"
"Schram Auto Sealer Company,
Patd 1901, Waterloo, Ont."
"Schram Bottle Cap, Pat 1901
& 3, Mfd, for Gowens Kent & Co.,
Toronto"

"STAR" (Ground Lip)

Factory: Unknown, possibly the Sydenham Glass Company.

Am. Pint **$350**

Am. Quart **$30**

Am. Half-Gallon **$50**

"TRUE FRUIT Trade Mark Registered Canada" (Smooth Lip)

Factory: Dominion Glass Company.

Am. Half-Gallon **$50**

Note: The J. Hungerford Smith Co., Toronto produced and packed crushed fruit, fountain syrups and fruit flavouring extracts etc., and were suppliers to the restaurant and hotel trade.

"VACUUM" (Smooth Lip)

Factory: Lid embossed "Patented in Canada 1924 by Sager Glass Corp. Ltd., Toronto."

Am. Pint, Quart and Half-Gallon measure with lid and spring top.

$20 - $25

VACUUM PUMP

A pump was used to extract air from jars such as the one illustrated at left. When the contents had been processed a glass lid was fitted and a vacuum pump was placed over the jar. A rubber gasket on the pump sealed round the shoulder of the jar and when the handle was raised suction was created to remove the air. The distinct click that could be heard was an indication that the jar was sealed.

"MacLAREN'S IMPERIAL CHEESE"
Burlington Glass Works.
Clear, ht. 5" **$75**

The MacLaren's cheese jars were also made in opaque white.

Left:
"BOWES CHOCOLATE SYRUP"
74 oz. **$25**

Right:
"HARRY HORNE'S MELLO CREAM" 64 oz. **$15**

Above, left to right:
"FRENCH'S MEDFORD BRAND PREPARED MUSTARD" Pint **$10**

"WHITE STAR MIXED PICKLES" Quart **$25**

"WHITE STAR BAKING POWDER" Pint **$25**

Medicinals

EMBOSSED "DR. THOMAS" ECLECTRIC OIL"
ABM, screw top. Ht. 6"
With box **$15**

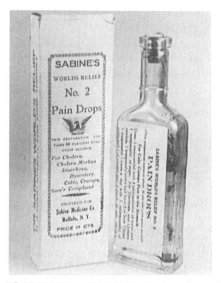

"SABINE'S PAIN DROPS" Buffalo, N.Y.
ABM, pink label and box. Ht. of box 6"
1920's. With box and original
instructions **$15**

"McELREE'S CARDUI"
A vegetable and alcohol bitters
tonic. Chattanooga Medicine Co.,
Chattanooga, Tenn.
Clear, ABM, 1930's. Ht. 7 1/2"
Bottle with contents and box **$15**

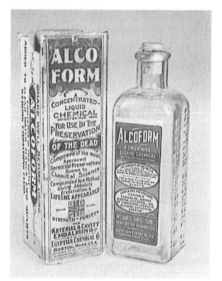

"ALCO FORM EMBALMING FLUID"
Egyptian Chemical Co.,
Boston, Mass.
Ht. of box 7" Ca. 1910.
With box **$15**

BOTTLES WITH CONTENTS - BIMAL Left to Right:

"REXALL PILE REMEDY" United Drug Co., Toronto **$10**

"SWAIZEMA" C.E. Swaisland, Kitchener. Ht. 7 1/2" **$15**

"MONTSERRAT EFFERVESCENT SALT" Montserrat Co., Montreal **$15**

"SEN-OIL" The Druggist's Corp. of Canada, Toronto **$10**

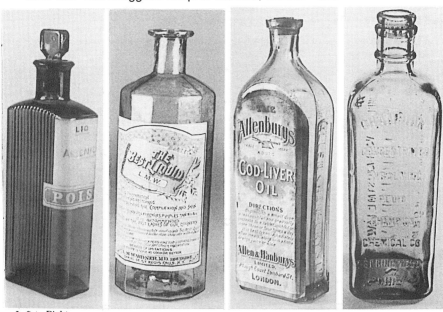

Left to Right:

POISON BOTTLE. Emerald green, ABM. Original stopper. Ht. 6" **$25**

"THE BEST LIQUID" Complexion treatment by Dr. L.M. Wardner, St. Regis Falls, N.Y. Clear, BIMAL, Ca. 1870's Ht. 7" **$20**

"ALLENBURY'S COD-LIVER OIL" Embossed and labelled. ABM. 1920's. Ht. 9 1/2" **$10**

EMBOSSED "Champion Embalming Fluid, Champion Chemical Co., Springfield, Ohio" Clear, ABM. Early 1900's. Ht. 8" **$20**

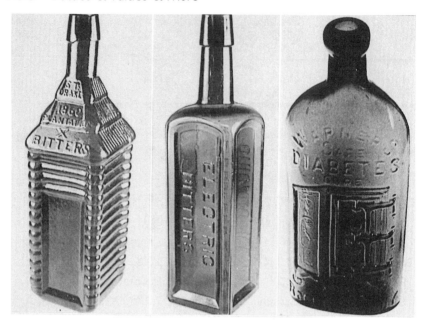

Left to Right:

EMBOSSED "S.T. Drake 1860 Plantation Bitters" Amber, BIMAL **$75**

EMBOSSED "Electric Bitters" Amber, BIMAL. Ht. 9" **$50**

EMBOSSED "Warner's Safe Diabetes Cure" Amber, BIMAL. Ht. 9 1/2" **$100**

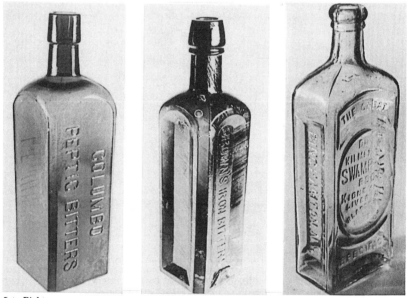

Left to Right:

EMBOSSED "Columbo Peptic Bitters" Amber, BIMAL. Ht. 9" **$40**

EMBOSSED "Brown's Iron Bitters" Amber, BIMAL. Ht. 9" **$25**

EMBOSSED "Dr. Kilmer's Swamp Root" Aqua, BIMAL. Ht. 8" **$20**

Left to Right:
EMBOSSED "Dr. Mill's New Heart Cure" Aqua, BIMAL. Ht. 8 1/4" **$35**

EMBOSSED "Haskin's Nervine" Aqua, BIMAL. Ht. 9" **$20**

EMBOSSED "C. Gates & Co., Life of Man Bitters" Clear, BIMAL. Ht. 8" **$60**

Left to Right:
EMBOSSED "Domestic Specialty Co., Hamilton, Ont." Aqua, BIMAL. **$5**

EMBOSSED "Burdock Blood Bitters" Aqua, BIMAL. Ht. 8 1/2" **$5**

EMBOSSED "Dr. Laviolette's Syrup of Turpentine" Clear, BIMAL. Ht. 4 1/2" **$8**

SNUFF BOTTLE.
Blown, dark olive green octagonal, no mould marks. Parchment colour label, Ca. 1840. Ht. 4" **$40**

EMBOSSED
"Lyon's Powder" Bed bug powder bottles. BIMAL, late 1800's. Ht. 4 1/2" Amber and green. **Each $40**

Left:
BLOWN MEDICINALS.
Aqua, late 1800's.
Height of tallest 6 1/2"
Each $25

EYE CUPS - British Left to Right:
Peacock blue **$40;** Jade green **$40;** Turquoise slag **$40;**
Custard **$40;** Lavender **$40;** Cobalt blue **$25.**

Soda & Pop Bottles

There are several versions given of the origin of soda water and the beginnings of the soft drink industry.

Originally the chemists in Europe were endeavouring to produce something to equal the effervescent waters of the famous mineral springs, because of their therapeutic value. It was Jan Baptista van Helmont (1577-1644) who used the term "gas" when he referred to the carbon dioxide content. Later it was termed "aerated water" by Gabriel Vanel who confused the gas with ordinary air. Another experimenter Joseph Black, called it "fixed air."

Before long factories and bottling plants were opened right across Europe and by 1807 Benjamin Silliman of Yale College in Connecticut was producing bottled "Soda Water" in the U.S.A. Joseph Hawkins of Philadelphia designed his own machinery and the firm of Shaw and Hawkins was established around 1809. This machinery was actually an improvement of the Schweppes patent process, which had been in operation since 1792.

It was Richard Bewley of England who hit on the idea of adding flavour and in 1768 offered to the public "mephitic julep," which was taken with a draft of lemonade. Soon there were three definite types of beverages: The 'natural' mineral waters, soda waters and flavoured carbonated drinks.

In Ireland the credit for soda water is given to Augustine Thwaites. In the history of Cantrell and Cochrane, famous Dublin soft drink firm, there is this statement:

"Soda water was invented by Augustine Thwaites who had an apothecary shop in Dublin. In 1769 he discovered that he could produce an effervescent water containing soda. Together with his son he formed a partnership and they produced Single and Double Soda Waters. The bottles which they used were rounded and pointed. The corks were wired in place to keep them moist and to prevent them from coming out since the gas pressure was such that the corks would pop out unless secured. The firm was later taken over by Cantrell and Cochrane and later Cochrane's name only appeared on the bottles."

In Australia the credit is given to Nicholas Paul, a Swiss, who invented "a glass bottle of an oval shape with stout walls" in 1790. This bottle was termed a "drunken bottle," since it was not possible to stand it up. In England in 1814 a Mr. Hamilton designed 'torpedo' bottles for Schweppe & Co.

Wm. H. Glendinning of Dartmouth was the first manufacturer of soft drinks in Nova Scotia, possibly just prior to 1836. R.A. Pilgrim of Hamilton was producing these drinks in Ontario in 1848. Alex Phillips of the Pioneer Soda Water Works of Victoria, B.C. was the first in western Canada, ca. 1858.

Right across Canada, as in America, Europe and Australia, the soft drink industry spread and every town of any size had a manufacturer of a social beverage, which had started in the sixteenth century as a likely medicine.

Embossed Soda & Pop Bottles

"H.W. GLENDINNING, Halifax, Nova Scotia" Aqua. BIMAL. **$300**

"WHELAN & FERGUSON, Halifax, N.S." Clear. BIMAL. **$45**

"J. MUSSON, Quebec" Aqua. BIMAL. $200

"KENNETH CAMPBELL & CO., Medical Hall, Montreal" Aqua. BIMAL. **$50**

"C. GURD & CO., Montreal" Aqua. BIMAL. **$85**

"J. EVES SODA WATER MANR., Toronto" Aqua. BIMAL. **$250**

"JNO VERNER TORONTO" Aqua. BIMAL. **$25**

"KNOX BROS., Belleville" Aqua. BIMAL. **$75**

"JOHN SMART, Owen Sound" Aqua. BIMAL. **$80**

"W. PIPE, Kingston" Aqua. BIMAL. **$95**

"IMPERIAL, Hamilton" Aqua. BIMAL. **$75**

Left to Right:

"BEAVER SODA WATER WORKS,
A & W Burns, 422 Yonge St., Toronto" Aqua. BIMAL. **$50**

"BEAVER SODA WATER WORKS,
A & W Burns, 406 Yonge St., Toronto" Aqua. BIMAL. **$60**

"WALSH & WILLERTON, Toronto"
Aqua. BIMAL. Slight damage. **$65**

"IMPERIAL SODA WATER WORKS,
Walsh & Co., 48 Richmond St. E., Toronto" Aqua. BIMAL. **$60**

Left to Right:

"J. EVES SODA WATER MANR"
"This bottle is never sold"
Dated "1862"
Aqua. BIMAL. **$100**

"WM. PIPE, Kingston, C.W."
Aqua. BIMAL. **$250**

"PERRIN'S CITY POPWORKS, London, C.W."
Aqua. BIMAL. **$250**

Above: Left to Right:

"R.A. PILGRIM & CO., Hamilton, C.W."
On reverse, eagle and trade mark. Aqua. BIMAL. **$140**

"H.W. BILTON SODA WATER MANR."
On reverse, "Trademark Registered 1868" Aqua. BIMAL. **$60**

"WALSH & CO., 124 Berkeley St., Toronto"
Aqua. BIMAL. **$150**

Below: Left to Right:

"MILTON AERATED WATER WORKS, Queens Co., N.S."
Clear. Codd stopper **$60**

"W.E. RUMMINGS, Nanaimo, B.C."
Aqua. Inside thread **$45**

Left to Right:
"PAXTON & CO., Port Perry"
Aqua. BIMAL. **$100+**
"JOHN WARMINTON, Port Hope"
Aqua. BIMAL **$125+**

Left to Right:
"R. TAYLOR, Strathroy"
Aqua. BIMAL. **$50**
"JOHN VERNER, Toronto"
Aqua. BIMAL. **$30**

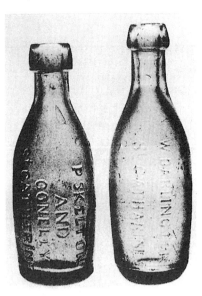

Left to Right:
"B. HYNES, St. Catharines" Aqua. BIMAL. **$45**

"NICHOLSON & McNULTY, St. Catharines" Aqua. BIMAL. **$60**

"P. SKELTON AND CONELLY, St. Catherines" (note mis-spelling)
Aqua. BIMAL. **$100+**

"W. DARLINGTON, St. Catharines" Aqua. BIMAL. **$100+**

Above: Left to Right:

"J. CHRISTIN & CO., Montreal"
Aqua. BIMAL. **$50**

"R.J. GARNETT, 122 Brussels St., St. John, N.B."
Aqua. BIMAL. **$50**

"WILLIAM CIVAN, Moncton, N.B."
Aqua. BIMAL. **$45**

"FARQUHAR & WILSON, Established 1845, Montreal"
Aqua. BIMAL. **$85 STAND $20**

Left to Right:

"S. BELCH, Belleville, C.W."
Green. BIMAL. **$245**

"CLARKE BROS., Toronto"
Aqua. BIMAL. **$40**

Above: Left to Right:

"ONTARIO SODA WATER WORKS, J.C. Wesley, Whitby"
Aqua. BIMAL. **$150**

"BABY & HANRAHAN, Windsor"
Pale green. BIMAL. **$65**

"JAS. McGUIRE, Stirling, Ont."
Aqua. BIMAL **$200**

"TOSSELL'S LAGER BEER & GINGER ALE, Niagara Falls"
Aqua. BIMAL. **$100**

Left to Right:

"W. CROFT, Peterboro"
Aqua. BIMAL. **$75**

"PILGRIM BROS & CO., Hamilton"
Green. BIMAL. **$100**

Left to Right: **"PILGRIM BROS., Hamilton"** Aqua. BIMAL. **$60**

"T.A. NICHOLSON, St. Catharines" Aqua. BIMAL. **$60**

"T. ROBERTSON, St. Catharines" Aqua. BIMAL. **$60**

"ST. KITTS BOTTLING WORKS, J. Gallagher" (St. Catharines) Clear. ABM. **$30**

Left to Right: **"SAUGEEN MINERAL WATER, Southampton"** Aqua. BIMAL. **$100**

"W. GARFAT, Port Hope" Aqua. BIMAL. **$70**

"A.W. BROWN, Brampton" Aqua. BIMAL. **$80**

Left to right:

"J. TUNE & SON, London, Ont."
Aqua. BIMAL. **$47**

"JAMES THOMPSON, Kingston"
Clear. BIMAL. **$75**

Left to right:

"THE WENTWORTH MINERAL WATER CO. LTD., Hamilton"
Aqua. BIMAL. **$40**

"F.J. YOUNG, Woodstock"
Aqua. BIMAL. **$40**

Left to right:

"THE RUSSEL MINERAL WATER CO. LTD., Clarence Creek, Ont."
Clear BIMAL. **$55**

"J.W. SUTHERLAND, Hamilton"
Aqua. BIMAL. **$20**

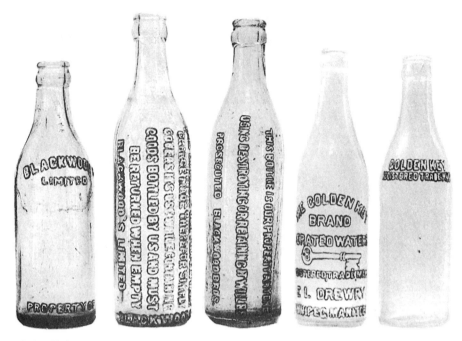

Left to Right:
"BLACKWOOD'S LIMITED" (Winnipeg, Man.) Aqua. BIMAL.   **$20**
"BLACKWOOD'S LIMITED" (Winnipeg, Man.) Aqua. ABM.   **$18**
"BLACKWOOD'S LIMITED" (Winnipeg, Man.) Clear. BIMAL.   **$25**
"THE GOLDEN KEY BRAND" (Winnipeg, Man.) Clear. BIMAL.   **$30**
"GOLDEN KEY" (Winnipeg, Man.) Aqua. BIMAL   **$22**

Left to Right:
"REGINA AERATED WATER COMPANY, Regina, Sask." Aqua. ABM.   **$25**

"ESTEVAN BOTTLING WORKS, Estevan, Sask." Clear. ABM.   **$30**

"STANDARD AERATED WATER CO., Arcola, Sask." Clear. ABM.   **$38**

Left:

"SUTHERLAND'S LIMITED, Hamilton"

Aqua. ABM. **$20**

Right:

"CANADIAN SODA WATER MFG. CO. Hamilton"

Aqua. ABM. **$25**

Above:

"ST. LEON MINERAL WATER CO. LTD., St. Leon, Quebec"

Aqua. BIMAL. **$50**

Left:

"CUMMER & SON, Hamilton"

Green. ABM. **$35**

Right:

"KAWARTHA DRINKS, Peterboro"

Green. ABM. **$40**

a   b   c   d   e

Left to right:

a) "SAUGEEN MINERAL WATER/SOUTHAMPTON."

Has a logo of a kneeling Indian. Clear, split, applied crown top. Has internal stain, light external scratches. Has a 2 1/8" crack at base. Along with a "WALSH & CO TORONTO" squat soda, which has a body crack and is stained. **$20**

b) Hutchinson Bottle. "WILLIAM TAYLOR/OWEN SOUND."

Aqua. Has internal stain and external scratches. Base embossed "WT." **$20**

c) "JNO VERNER/TORONTO."

Has Beaver logo, is deep aqua, stained and scratches. Dug condition. Base embossed "V." **$15**

"CLARK BROS/TOROTNO."

Aqua, stained and scratched. Dug condition. Base embossed "C." **$15**

d) "THOS. TUNE & CO/ STRATFORD"

Aqua, overall light internal stain. Light overall external stain. Dug condition. **$24**

e) "LA KIRKLAND/lion logo/ TORONTO."

Pint, aqua, ABM. Has light internal stain, light external scratches. Dug condition. Base embossed "K." **$7**

Canada Dry

John J. McLaughlin, chemist, of Toronto, Ontario, manufactured carbonated beverages in 1890. In 1894 a modern plant was built in Toronto and is still in operation. In 1908 a new ginger ale formula was evolved and placed on the market as "Canada Dry." This proved so popular that the firm built a factory in Edmonton, Alberta, in 1907.

The business was incorporated in 1912 under the name of J.J. McLaughlin Ltd. The sale of Canada Dry in the U.S.A. was begun in 1922 by Canada Dry Ginger Ale Inc., New York, N.Y., producing 500 cases of 50 bottles per day. By 1923 the sales had increased to 103,000 cases per day and a new factory was purchased at Hudson, N.Y.

In Dec. 1923 the issued capital stock of J.J. McLaughlin Ltd. was sold to Canada Dry Ginger Ale Inc., which became the holding company. Later the Corporation acquired Caledonia Springs (Canada) Ltd., G.B. Seeley's Sons Inc., Chelmsford Ginger Ale (U.S.A.) Inc.

Facts from "Financial Review" 1932

Left to Right:

"HYGEIA WATERS, J.J. McLaughlin, Chemist, Toronto" Clear. BIMAL. **$100**

"HYGEIA WATERS, J.J. McLaughlin, Chemist, Toronto" Aqua. BIMAL. **$30**

"McLAUGHLIN'S HYGEIA WATERS, Toronto" Clear. BIMAL. **$75**

"THIS BOTTLE THE PROPERTY OF J.J. McLAUGHLIN, Ottawa." Pale green. ABM. **$30**

Above, left to right:

"CANADA DRY"
Iridescent golden amber. ABM. **$22**

"CANADA DRY"
Green. ABM. Paper label. **$15**

"CANADA DRY"
Green. ABM. Paper label. **$30**

"CANADA DRY"
Green. ABM. Paper label.
75th anniversary bottle. **$10**

Left:

"DUNCAN WATER"
The Caledonia Springs Company,
Caledonia Springs, Ont.
Cobalt blue. BIMAL. Paper label. **$25**

Charles Wilson Ltd.

Charles Wilson's career began as an apprentice at the ginger ale bottling works of Mrs. Farquhar in Montreal in 1850. The partnership of Farquhar & Wilson was eventually formed and by 1867 Charles Wilson had established his own business.

Wilson's moved to Toronto in 1875 and set up a business to manufacture ginger ales and mineral waters. At the 1876 International Exhibition, Philadelphia, Pa., Wilson products, ginger ale and mineral water, were awarded a certificate and medal. On May 3rd 1969 after over ninety years at one location, Sherbourne St., Toronto, a new bottling plant was opened at Duncan Mills Road in Don Mills, Ontario.

Charles Wilson Ltd. was purchased by Crush International in 1973, production of Wilson's products continued until mid 1985.

"CHARLES WILSON: LATE OF MONTREAL"
On reverse, "Toronto" Aqua. BIMAL.   **$50**

"CHAS. WILSON, Toronto, Ont."
On reverse, squirrel trade mark.
Aqua. BIMAL.   **$45**

"WILSON'S"
"Diamond Jubilee
Dry Ginger Ale" 1935.
Green. ABM.
Paper label.   **$9**

Above, left to right:

"CHAS. L. HORSMAN, Cambellford, Ont."
Note mis-spelling of Campbellford.
Clear. ABM.   **$40**

"VESS DRY"
Green bar shaker with screw top.   **$40**

"ORANGE SWEET BOTTLING CO., Toronto"
Clear ABM.   **$10**

Left to Right:

"JUMBO" Jumbo Beverages Co.
Clear. ABM.   **$25**

"MAMMY" Mammy Beverages Co.
Clear ABM.   **$25**

Left to right:
"WISHING WELL" Clear. ABM. **$10**
"ORANGE DANDY" Clear. ABM. **$10**
"RED WING ORCHARDS" Clear. ABM. **$25**
"CROWN BOTTLING WORKS, Port Hope" Clear. ABM. **$8**

Left to right:
"MacDONALD'S NATURAL FLAVOUR BEVERAGES" Clear. ABM. **$10**
"CRONMILLER GINGER ALE, Port Colborne" Clear. ABM. **$10**
"ORANGE QUENCH, Owen Sound" Clear. ABM. **$10**
"ORANGE CRUSH" Pale green. ABM. **$10**
"ORANGE CRUSH" Pale green. ABM. **$11**
"ORANGE CRUSH" Pale green. ABM. **$30**

Left to right:
"JERSEY CREME COMPANY, Toronto" Clear. ABM. **$20**
"WHISTLE" Clear. ABM. **$20**
"ONTARIO SODA WATER CO., Toronto, Ont." Clear. ABM. **$20**
"KIST" Clear. ABM. **$8**
"KIST" Clear. ABM. **$30**

Left to right:
"QUENCH"
 Clear. ABM. **$15**
"WENTWORTH"
Clear. ABM. **$20**
"EVANGELINE"
Clear. ABM. **$7**

Left to Right:

"EXCELSIOR BOTTLING WORKS LTD., Toronto"
Clear. ABM. **$10**

"FRUIT SQUEEZE, Dominion Soda Water Works"
Clear. ABM. **$8**

"HAMBLY BEVERAGES, Oshawa"
Clear. ABM. **$8**

Left to Right:

"FLIRT" Clear. ABM. **$10**

"LINDSAY SODA WATER WORKS" Clear. ABM. **$10**

"KAYO CHOCOLATE" Clear. ABM. **$8**

"WHISTLE BEVERAGES" Clear. ABM. **$7**

"KUNTZ'S BEVERAGES" Clear. ABM. **$14**

Left to right:

"PARIS SODA WATER MFG. CO., Montreal" Aqua. BIMAL. **$75**

"ROWAN BROS. & CO., Montreal" Aqua. ABM. **$25**

"CHAS. GURD, Montreal, Aqua. ABM. **$40**

"PETERSON'S LIMITED, Toronto. Aqua. ABM. **$15**

Left to right:

"CRESCENT BOTTLING WORKS, Fort William"
Clear. ABM. **$12**

"COBALT AERATED WATER CO."
Clear. BIMAL. **$20**

"SPRING WATER BOTTLING WORKS, Niagara Falls South, Ont."
Clear. ABM. **$14**

Left to right:

"FELIX J. QUINN, Halifax, N.S." Aqua. BIMAL. **$20**

"FELIX J. QUINN, Halifax, N.S." Aqua. BIMAL. **$25**

"FELIX J. QUINN, Halifax, N.S." Aqua. BIMAL. **$30**

"JAS ROUE, Halifax, N.S." Aqua. BIMAL. **$30**

"JAS ROUE, Halifax, N.S." Aqua. Blop Top. **$35**

Left to right:

"JAS ROUE, Halifax, N.S."
Aqua, BIMAL. **$20**

**"SUSSEX MINERAL
SPRINGS, Sussex, N.B."**
Clear. ABM. **$25**

**"SUSSEX BEVERAGE
COMPANY"**
Clear. ABM. **$30**

"Pop" Bottles with Paper Labels

Left to Right:

"TEXAS PUNCH"	$12
"TOM COLLINS"	$12
"PENGUIN GINGER ALE"	$12

Left to Right:

"RED & WHITE GINGER ALE"	$7.50
"ALPINE GINGER ALE"	$7.50
"DOMINO"	$7.50

Left to Right:

"ROYAL CHARGER JUICY ORANGE"	$10
"ROYAL CHARGER GINGER ALE"	$10

Not Shown:

"BLACKWOOD'S DRY GINGER ALE" Winnipeg, Manitoba. Green. ABM. 7 oz. Paper label. **$10**

"McLAUGHLINS GINGER ALE" Aqua. ABM. 7 oz. Paper label. **$10**

"PREMIER LEMON SOUR" Brandon, Manitoba. Aqua. ABM. 7 oz. Paper label. **$12**

"10/10 DRY GINGER ALE" Green. ABM. 30 oz. Paper label. **$8**

"VARISTY BRAND DRY GINGER ALE" Edmonton, Alberta. Aqua. ABM. 7 oz. Paper label. **$10**

Above, left to right:

"2-WAY" Brighton Bottling Works, Brighton, Ont. Amber. ABM. **$8**

"SPARKLING LEMON SOUR" R.H. Martin, Lindsay, Ont. Green. ABM. **$20**

"PALE DRY GINGER ALE" John Crimmons, Lindsay, Ont. Green. ABM. **$12**

"DREWRY'S CRYSTAL SODA" E.L. Drewry Ltd., Winnipeg, Man. Green. ABM. **$10**

Left to right:

"O'KEEFE'S GINGER ALE" Green. ABM. **$20**

"O'KEEFE'S LIME RICKEY" Green. ABM. **$20**

"Pop" Bottles with Applied Coloured Labels

APPLIED COLOURED LABELS (ACL)

A labelling process, using a coloured paste applied through a steel screen and fired. Developed in the U.S. during the 1920's and came into popular use during the '30's on milk and soft drink bottles.

Above, left to right:
"KIK" $2; "KIK" $20; "KIK" $5

Left to right:
"SHORTY" $40
"SHORTY" $20
"VICTORIA DRY GINGER ALE" $10
"BIG GIANT COLA" $10

Left to right:
"BARREL OF BEVERAGE" $12
"STUBBY" $10
"STUBBY" $10
"DONALD DUCK COLA" $15

Left to right:
"ROBINSON'S GINGER ALE" **$4**
"GARLAND'S BEVERAGES" **$8**
"BELL CITY BEVERAGES" **$4**

Not Shown:
"American Dry"
Green. ABM. 30 oz. ACL. **$8 - $10**

Left to right:
"KIST" **$15**
"KIST" **$8**
"FESTIVAL DRY" **$6**
"FESTIVAL DRY" **$10**

Not Shown:
"DELICIOUS VITALITY SOFT DRINKS"
Clear. ABM. 10 oz. ACL. **$4**

Left to right:
"WINOLA" **$12**
"SILVER FOAM" **$20**
"KIST" **$8**

Left to right:
"OLD COLONY" **$4**
"OLD COLONY" **$6**
"OLD COLONY" **$4**

Left to right:
"DOMINION BEVERAGES" $6
"VERNORS" $6
"WHISTLE" $6

Not shown:
"DELUXE BEVERAGES"
 Green. ABM. 30 oz. ACL.   **$10**

Left to right:
"BEL BOY BEVERAGES" $10
"EVANGELINE" $5
"HAMILTON BEVERAGES" $8

Not shown:
**"DOMINION DRY
GINGER ALE CO."**
Green. ABM. 30 oz.
ACL.   **$10**
"GURDS"
Green. ABM. 30 oz.
ACL.   **$7**
"GURDS"
Green. ABM. 10 oz.
ACL.   **$5**
"GURDS"
Green. ABM. 7 oz.
ACL.   **$4**

Left to right:
**"RENFREW
FLAVOURS"
$4.50**
"McGIRR'S" $5
"MacDONALDS" $7
"SILVER FOAM" $6

$10 $10

$5 $12

$10 $12

$7 $12 $7

Left to right:

"MORAN BEVERAGES" $10

"STUBBY" $10

"PICK 'N DRINK" $10

Not Shown:

"JAMAICA DRY GINGER ALE"
Green ABM. 10 oz. ACL. **$10**

"JERSEY DRY BEVERAGES"
Green. ABM. 30 oz. ACL. **$8**

"THE POP PEOPLE"
Clear. ABM. 10 oz. ACL. **$3**

"REGAL BEVERAGES"
Clear. ABM. 10 oz. ACL. **$4**

"RUMMY"
Green. ABM. 7 oz. ACL. **$5**

"SUNNYSIDE BEVERAGES"
Green. ABM. 10 oz. ACL. **$6**

Left to right:

"TRUDELS BEVERAGES" $12

"PURE SPRING" $12

$6	$6	$6	$6	$6

NOTE: The decorative applied coloured labels on pop and beverage bottles were designed with colourful logos and crests etc. Examples of this type of bottle which may be found, with variations, across Canada are illustrated and priced here.

$10	$12	$10	$10

Left:
"2-WAY Brighton Bottling Works, Brighton, Ont."
Amber **$8**

Right:
"DREWRY'S CRYSTAL SODA."
E.L. Drewry Ltd., Winnipeg, Man.
Green. **$10**

Left:
"O'KEEFE'S GINGER ALE."
Green. **$20**
Right:
"O'KEEFE'S LIME RICKEY."
Green **$20**

Left to right:
"CHOCOLATE SOLDIER" $10
"STAR BEVERAGES" $5
"COLLINS" $6
"1 CAL" $5
"SQUIRT" $5

Left to right:
"SUN CREST" $4
"STUBBY" $6

Left to right:
"HOWDY" $3
"TONA-COLA" $5
"NU-GRAPE" $6
"BASTIEN'S" $6

Pepsi-Cola

Pharmacist, Caleb Bradburn of New Bern, North Carolina, was the originator of the first Pepsi-Cola formula. At the time, 1896, the beverage was unnamed, the name Pepsi-Cola was registered as a trademark in 1903. By 1916 one hundred bottling franchises had been issued as the popularity of this beverage began to spread to the rest of the country. Today, Pepsi-Cola is bottled and sold in over 100 countries around the world.

"**PEPSI-COLA**" Celluloid over tin sign. 11 1/2" x 8"   **$145**

Left:
"Bottled under special appointment by J.W. Boorman, Peterborough."
$20

Right:
"Bottled under special appointment by Chas L. Horsman, Campbellford."
$25

Note: Both bottles have paper labels.

"**PEPSI-COLA**" Miniature bottle with original cap.   **$26**

Pop "Go-Withs"

STORE DOOR PUSH BARS. Length 31 1/2"
"SCHWEPPES" $50
"PEPSI-COLA" $40
"UP-TOWN" $40

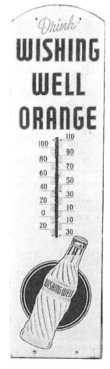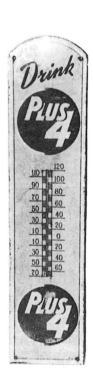

THERMOMETERS: Left to Right:
"WISHING WELLS" Tin $100; "ORANGE KIST" Wood $150
"PLUS-4" Tin $75

Left to right:
"7-UP" Tin sign, 53" x 17"   **$150**
"7-UP" Tin thermometer, 14" x 6"   **$150**
"ORANGE CRUSH" Wood sign, 39" x 8 1/2"   **$125**

"TEEM" Tin sign, 19" x 27"   **$95**

Above: left:
"HONEE-ORANGE"
Tin sign, 29" x 29" **$85**

Above: right:
"HIRES" Tin menu board.
15 1/2" x 29 1/2" **$85**

Left:
"STUBBY"
Tin sign, 27" x 19" **$75**

"NIAGARA PUNCH" Tin sign, 9 1/4" x 19 1/2" **$100**

Coca-Cola

The "Coca-Cola" trademark has been used by the Coca-Cola Company since 1886. They have always advertised extensively to sell their products world-wide. Collectors of "Coke" bottles have an almost unlimited selection of items bearing the "Coca-Cola" or "Coke" trademark to choose from. A selection of "Go-Withs" is illustrated in this section.

Note:

Until 1955 Coca-Cola was available in 6 1/2 oz. bottles or by the glass at soda fountains. Beginning in 1955 Coke was packaged in 10, 12, 16 and 26 oz. bottles and 12 oz. cans were being market tested by the armed forces. In 1960 cans of Coca-Cola were available to consumers. During the 1970's 32, 48 and 64 oz. bottles of Coke were introduced and in 1977 the plastic 2 litre size was made available.

EARLY BOTTLES. Left to Right:
"Coca-Cola" at bottom. 1900.   **$40**
"Coca-Cola" in middle. 1930.   **$40**
"Coca-Cola" at top. 1906.   **$40**

AMBER COCA-COLA BOTTLES WITH ARROWS.

Left:
Circular arrow, 1905.   **$100**

Right:
Straight arrow, 1907.**$100**

Chronology of the Glass Package for Coca-Cola 1894 – 1975

1894   1899–1902   1900 ——— 1916   1915

1923   1937   1957   1961   Plastic 1975

Courtesy of The Coca-Cola Company

Previous page – top row, left to right:

1894   Hutchinson bottle embossed "Biedenharn Candy Co."
         The first bottler of Coca-Cola

1899 – 1902   Hutchinson bottle embossed "Coca-Cola"

1900 – 1916   Straight sided bottles with crown closures.
         Clear and amber with diamond shaped paper labels.

1915   "Mae West" or hobble skirt bottle, patented Nov. 16.

Previous page – bottom row, left to right:

1923   Christmas bottle, patented Dec. 25.

1937   Patent No. D-105529

1957   Applied coloured label.

1961   No return, one way bottle.

1975   Experimental plastic package. Tested 1970 - 75.

SODA WATER BOTTLES. Property of Coca-Cola Company. Left to right:

Pale green. 1920's - 30's. **$45**

Clear. 1920's - 30's. **$45**

Pale green. 1920's - 30's **$45**

GOLD SEAL. Property of Coca-Cola Company. Left to right:

Clear, Ca. 1925 **$25**

Clear, Ca. 1925 **$25**

Left to Right:

MAE WEST COCA-COLA BOTTLE.
Patented Nov. 15, 1916. **$100**

COCA-COLA BOTTLE.
Patented Dec. 25, 1923. **$55**

COCA-COLA BOTTLE. 1958 **$10**

COCA-COLA BOTTLE.
1958. "D" in diamond at base. **$10**

COCA-COLA CANS. Above, left to right:
Canadian. 1962 **$45 - $50**

Canadian. 1962. **$45 - $50**

Anniversary Can. "Florida Bottling Co., Daytona Beach, 1902 - 1977, 75 years of refreshment" **$10**

Left:

COKE. Clear with applied coloured label.
Introduced 1957. **$5**

**COCA-COLA
ANNIVERSARY BOTTLE.**
With contents and original cap. **$25**

Left:
GOLD COCA-COLA BOTTLE.
Ca. 1949. **$130**

Right:
**EXPERIMENTAL
COCA-COLA BOTTLE.**
Greenish amber. Ca. 1958. **$20**

COMMEMORATIVE BOTTLE.
Royal Wedding Prince Charles
and Lady Diana, July 29, 1981.
Twist cap, no deposit.
250 ml. **$100**

**MINIATURE PROMOTIONAL
COCA-COLA BOTTLES.**
Clear. Ht. 2 1/2"
Each $15

ONE WAY, NO DEPOSIT COCA-COLA BOTTLES.
Introduced 1961. 7 oz to 16 oz. **Each $10**

COCA-COLA BOTTLES CAPS. Mounted on board under cellophane.
1964 - 65 National Hockey League Players. Six teams: Montreal Canadiens, Boston Bruins; New York Rangers; Toronto Maple Leafs, Chicago Black Hawks and Detroit Red Wings. Boards to mount cap with each players picture could be picked up at gas stations etc.
14 1/2" x 23" **Complete set $250**

Coca Cola "Go-Withs"

ELECTRIC CLOCK.
Enamelled tin, red centre, brown surround with gold numerals. American. 1961. Diam. 17" **$90**

Left:
STORE REGULATOR.
By the E. Ingraham Clock Co., Bristol, Conn. 1905 - 07. 8-day, time only. Refinished oak case. 17 1/2" x 38 1/2" **$2,000**

Above:
ELECTRIC CLOCK.
Internally lit with florescent bulb. Metal casing with lucite. 1960's. 17" x 25 1/2" **$200**

Left:
ELECTRIC CLOCK.
Internally lit with two bulbs. Reverse painted on glass. 1960's. 15 1/4" x 15 1/4" **$150**

QUARTZ CLOCK. In picture frame. Scene with country store on canvas. Only 60 made. 1980's. 13" x 19" **$200**

Right:
ELECTRIC CLOCK. Internally lit with florescent bulb. Molded lucite. Ca. 1960's. 14 1/2" x 25" **$150**

Left:
ELECTRIC CLOCK. 1959. 15" x 15" **$150**

Right:
THERMOMETER.
Norman Rockwell illustration. 1980's. Diam. 12" **$30**

THERMOMETER.
Red dial. 1950. Diam. 12" **$125**

THERMOMETER.
Red dial. 1981. Diam. 12" **$25**

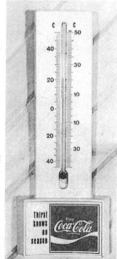
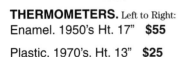

THERMOMETERS. Left to Right:
Enamel. 1950's Ht. 17" **$55**

Plastic. 1970's. Ht. 13" **$25**

Not shown:
Enamel bottle shaped thermometer, celsius. Mid 1970's - 1980's.
Ht. 15 1/2" **$45**

Left to right:
Enamel. 1939. Ht. 18" **$125**

Enamel. Lillian Russell. 1971.
Ht. 15 1/2" **$45**

Left to Right:

TIN SIGN. Ca. 1930's. 19" x 54" **$300**

ENAMEL SIGN. Ca. 1939. Ht. 54" **$225**

TIN SIGN. Ca. 1947. 16" x 40" **$200**

DISC/BUTTON SIGN. 1950's.
Diam. 24" **$150**

FLANGE SIGN. Ca. 1940's.
15 1/2" x 20" **$125**

Flanged at right angle so sign could be
fixed to side of building and be visible
from both sides.

Left:
SIGN. Celluloid
over tin. Ca. 1923.
5 3/4" x 11 3/4" **$175**

Right:
TIN SIGN. Full colour.
Ca. 1923. 19" x 27"
$300

Left:
ENAMEL SIGN. Ca. 1938.
19" x 28" **$250**

Right:
ENAMEL SIGN.
1950's 19" x 28"
Chipped $175

ENAMEL SIGN.
Ca. 1950. 12" x 28" **$150**

TIN SIGN. From the Atlanta, Georgia head office. Movie star Lupe Velez on left. Ice skater on right was featured on 1941 calendar, serving tray and poster. Ca. 1982. 24" x 33" **$100**

Above:
MENU BOARD. Chalkboard trimmed with porcelain on tin. 1950's. **$100**

Left:
MENU BOARD. Chalkboard trimmed with wood. 1950's. 24" x 30" **$125**

JIG-SAW PUZZLE. Lithographed in Canada. 1950's.12" x 18" Complete. **$165**

Above left:
JIG-SAW PUZZLE. 1901 Calendar girl. Full colour litho cardboard. 1960's. 11" x 14" With box. **$45**

Above right:
1951 CALENDAR. Full colour picture. Complete and mint. 13" x 22" **$65**

Below left:
1956 CALENDAR. Canadian. Complete. **$75**

WOOD 6-PACK BOTTLE CARRIER.
Late 1930's. Case only **$60**

WOOD 6-PACK BOTTLE CARRIER.
Late 1930's, early 1940's.
Case only **$55**

ALUMINUM 6-PACK BOTTLE CARRIER.
Late 1940's, early 1950's. Case only **$45**

DISPLAY RACK.
Cast iron base embossed "Property of Coca-Cola Canada." 1941.
Ht. 61" **$250**

MASONITE 6-PACK BOTTLE CARRIER.
1940's. **$45**

SODA JERK'S HAT Oil cloth.
Fair condition. **$65**
Mint condition. **$200**

BELL SHAPED GLASS
Applied lettering and lines.
1940's. Ht. 4" **$20 - $30**

Left to right:
GLASS DISPLAY BOTTLE.
Patented Dec. 25, 1923. Ht. 20" **$195**

GLASS DISPLAY BOTTLE.
Clear with applied coloured lettering.
With contents and original cap. Ht. 20"
$125

FLARE SHAPED GLASS.
Possibly a re-issue of early
1900's glass. Ht. 3" **$10**

Left to Right:
PLASTIC JUG.
Red and white 1970's. **$10**

PLASTIC CUP.
Red and white. 1970's. **$1**

PLASTIC CONTAINER.
Red and white. 1970's.
Ht. handle up 12" **$15**

Left to Right:
WAXED PAPER CUP.
1976 **$5 - $6**

PLASTIC CUP.
On reverse
Roberto Ramos **$10**

WAXED PAPER CUP.
1983. **$4 - $5**

WAXED PAPER CUPS. Left to right:
Front and back of cup commemorating 60th birthday of
Mickey Mouse. From Disney World. 1988 **$5**

Famous Players Theatres. **$4 - $5**

Front and back of cup from the 1988 Winter Olympics,
Calgary, Alberta. **$6**

KEY RINGS
Can shaped key ring, lower left, is also a flashlight.
Values $6 - $15

BALL POINT PENS. Given to salesmen.

Left:

Black. Late 1970's. **$10**

Bottom:

Red cobra skin. Mid to late 1980's. **$20**

Right:

Chrome. Early 1960's. **$8**

ZIPPO LIGHTERS
$20 - $25

KEY RING.
Chrome with plated brass coke bottle. **$15**

GIFT SET.
Key ring, coaster, bottle opener and letter opener. Given to top retailers. 1988.
Set $100

AWARDS & INSIGNIA

Top Row: Driver's service awards set with simulated diamonds and rubies etc. with numerals indicating years of service. **Each $250**

Bottom Row: Three at left - driver's service awards, enamelled numerals. All rare **$100 - $350**

Two at right: Convention insignia **$50 - $75**

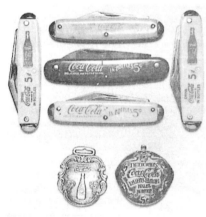

PEN KNIVES WITH PLASTIC HANDLES. Each $20

WATCH FOBS. Each $50

PULL-APART BOTTLE LIGHTERS. 1950's **Each $15**

TIFFANY STYLE LAMP.
Made for Canadian market,
English and French. Bronzed
metal base and stem. 1960's.
Ht. 25" Mint **$800**

ADJUSTABLE DESK LAMP.
Wood base, plastic shade. Early
1960's. Ht. 13" **$175**

CAN LIGHTER.
1950's - 1960's.
Ht. 6" **$75**

Left:
CAN/PHONE.
Working. 1980's.
Ht. 13" **$175**

Right:
BOTTLE/PHONE.
Working. 1984. **$25**

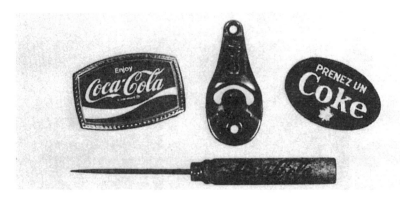

Left to right:
BELT BUCKLE **$10**

COUNTER BOTTLE OPENER **$25**

DELIVERY MAN'S JACKET CREST **$2.50**

ICE PICK **$8**

Back row, left to right:
SCHOOL BOOK COVER. 1930's **$10**

PENCIL CASE. With supplies. 1937. **$150**

BLOTTER. 1950's. **$20**

Front Row:
PLASTIC BALL POINT PENS. Each **$15**

EVERSHARP PENCIL. Wood, baseball bat shape. **$45**

RULER "The Coca-Cola Bottling Co." **$15**

RULER. "Drink Coca-Cola Iced" **$8**

YO-YO'S Early 1950's. **Each** **$45**

COCA-COLA NOVELTIES. Left to right:

Christmas ornament **$15**

Miniature camera. Working. **$10**

Tin box with playing cards and dice. **$20**

Thimble. Ruby glass. **$25**

Bell. Ruby glass. **$85**

Box of wood matches, tin cover. **$20**

COCA-COLA NOVELTIES Left to right:

Tin cup **$20**

Lighter **$20**

Six boxes of wood matches. **$35**

Sun glasses. Red and white. **$15**

Vending machine bank. Takes nickels, dispenses miniature bottles. **$40**

Litho-tin truck. **$35**

CAST IRON HORSE DRAWN COCA-COLA TRUCK WITH DRIVER.
Bottles in plastic cases. Late 1960's. **$150**

Right:
**CAST IRON
COCA-COLA TRUCK.**
Back doors open. 1960's.
L. 8 1/2" **$85**

COCA-COLA TRUCKS
Back: Metal and plastic by Buddy-L. 1950's Side lifts. L. 9" **$150**

Front, left to right: Plastic by Corgi. 1960's. **$65**

Plastic Leyland Terrier by Corgi. 1960's - 1970's. L. 3" **$35**

Plastic, no maker's name. 1960's. **$20**

COCA-COLA METAL TRAY
Ca. 1914. **$225**

GLASS COCA-COLA
20" high Display bottle **$95**

COCA-COLA DISPLAY SIGN
Made by the St. Thomas Sign
Company. Ca. 1948
19" x 54" **$225**

Serving & Change Trays

Trays were one of the many promotional methods used by the Coca-Cola Company to boost product awareness. Change and serving trays advertising "Delicious" and "Refreshing" "Coca-Cola" were first made in the late 1890's. Early serving trays were round measuring about 9 1/4" diameter, in 1905 large and medium size oval trays were introduced. Change trays were produced in various sizes, round from 4" to 6" diameter and oval 4 1/4" x 6." Production of change trays ceased in 1920.

From 1910 onwards a standard size was used for rectangular trays, 10 1/2" x 13 1/4", except in 1916 when a tray measuring 8 1/2" x 19" was issued and beginning in 1920 all trays were made in one shape – rectangular.

Production of trays ceased during both World Wars and after the second World War few trays were issued. "Recent trays" – commemoratives, T.V. trays and re-issues have been made since the 1950's.

Values are for trays in good to excellent condition.

GOOD - Picture, lettering and colour in good condition, minor scratches, flaking, fading, dents or rust.

EXCELLENT – Picture, lettering and colour in excellent condition, slight wear because of age or use.

SERVING TRAYS - Round & Oval

1897 Victorian Girl. Diam. 9 1/4"	**$5500 - $7000**
1899 Hilda Clark. Diam. 9 1/4"	**$5500 - $6500**
1900 Hilda Clark. Diam. 9 1/4"	**$3500 - $4000**
1901 Hilda Clark. Diam. 9 1/4"	**$2600 - $2800**
1903 Hilda Clark. Diam. 9 1/4"	**$2800 - $3000**
1903 Bottle Tray. Diam. 9 3/4"	**$4000 - $5000**
1905 Lillian Russell. Oval, 10 1/2" x 14 1/4"	**$1600 - $1800**
1906 Juanita. Oval. 10 1/2" x 13 1/4"	**$1000 - $1200**
1907 Relieves Fatigue. Oval. 10 1/2" x 13 1/4"	**$1000 - $1200**
1908 Topless Girl.	**$2000 - $2400**
1909 St. Louis Fair. Oval 13 1/2" x 16 1/2"	**$1300 - $1600**
1909 St. Louis Fair. Oval 10 1/2" x 13 1/4"	**$800 - $1000**
1913 Signed by Hamilton King. Oval, 12 1/2" x 15 1/4"	**$450 - $500**
1914 Betty. Oval, 12 1/2" x 15 1/4"	**$350 - $400**
1920 Garden Girl. Oval, 13 3/4" x 16 1/2"	**$575 - $650**

CHANGE TRAYS

1900 Hilda Clark. Diam. 6"	**$1800 - $2200**
1901 Hilda Clark. Diam. 6"	**$1100 - $1300**
1903 Hilda Clark. Diam. 6"	**$900 - $1050**
1903 Hilda Clark. Diam. 4"	**$750 - $800**
1903 Bottle Tray. Diam. 5 1/2"	**$2800 - $3200**
1906 Juanita. Diam. 4"	**$400 - $450**
1907 Relieves Fatigue. Oval, 4 1/4" x 6"	**$350 - $400**
1909 St. Louis Fair. Oval, 4 1/4" x 6"	**$250 - $300**
1910 Coca-Cola Girl. Oval. 4 1/4" x 6"	**$250 - $300**
1913 Signed by Hamilton King. Oval. 4 1/4" x 6"	**$250 - $300**
1916 Elaine. Oval. 4 1/4" x 6"	**$100 - $150**
1920 Garden Girl. Oval, 4 1/4" x 6"	**$250 - $300**

SERVING TRAYS. – Rectangular 10 1/2" x 13 1/4"

1910 Coca-Cola Girl	**$450 - $500**	1932 Bathing Beauty (on chair)	**$250 - $300**
1913 Signed by Hamilton King	**$375 - $450**	1933 Francis Dee	**$225 - $275**
1914 Betty	**$300 - $350**	1934 Maureen O'Sullivan & Johnny Weissmuler (illus.)	**$400 - $450**
1916 Elaine 8 1/2" x 19"	**$200 - $250**	1935 Madge Evans	**$175 - $200**
1920 Garden Girl	**$450 - $500**	1936 Hostess	**$175 - $200**
1921 Autumn Girl	**$400 - $475**	1937 Running Girl (illus.)	**$75 - $100**
1922 Summer Girl	**$400 - $450**	1938 Girl in the Afternoon (English)	**$70 - $85**
1923 Flapper Girl	**$225 - $250**	1938 Girl in the Afternoon (French) (illus.)	**$85 - $100**
1924 Smiling Girl	**$375 - $425**	1939 Springboard Girl	**$100 - $125**
1925 Girl at Party	**$225 - $275**	1940 Sailor Girl	**$100 - $125**
1926 Sports Couple (illus.)	**$300 - $375**	1941 Girl Ice Skater	**$100 - $125**
1927 Girl with Bobbed Hair	**$300 - $350**	1942 Two Girls at Car	**$75 - $100**
1927 Curb Service	**$300 - $325**	1948 Girl with Wind in Her Hair (Solid background)	**$75 - $100**
1928 Soda Fountain Clerk	**$275 - $300**	1948 Girl with Wind in Her Hair (Screened background, Eng.)	**$35 - $50**
1928 Girl in Swimsuit (with glass)	**$200 - $250**	1948 Girl with Wind in Her Hair (Screened, French, Illus.)	**$65 - $85**
1928 Girl in Swimsuit (with bottle)	**$250 - $300**		
1930 Girl with Telephone	**$175 - $200**		
1930 Bathing Beauty	**$175 - $200**		
1931 Farm Boy with Dog	**$350 - $400**		

Above right:

1934. Maureen O'Sullivan &
Johnny Weissmuler.   **$400 - $450**

Above left:

1926. Sports Couple.   **$300 - $375**

1937. Running Girl.
$75 - $100

1938. Girl in the Afternoon.
French   **$85 - $100**

1948. Girl with Wind in Her Hair.
Screen background, French.
$65 - $85

1950. Girl with Menu. French.
$45 - $65

1950's. Santa in Chair
with Boy & Girl. **$100 - $125**

1950's. Santa at Fireplace.
$100 - $125

1957. Rooster Tray.
$70 - $85

1958. Picnic Basket.
$15 - $25

1960's. Barefoot Boy.
$40 - $50

1960's. Old Oaken Bucket.
$40 - $50

SERVING TRAYS - Rectangular 10 1/2" x 13 1/4"

1950 Girl with Menu (English)	**$30 - $40**
1950 Girl with Menu (French) (illus.)	**$45 - $65**
1950's Santa in Chair with Boy & Girl (illus.)	**$100 - $125**
1950's Santa at Fireplace (illus.)	**$100 - $125**
1957 Birdhouse Tray (English)	**$65 - $80**
1957 Birdhouse Tray (French)	**$35 - $40**
1957 Rooster Tray (illus.)	**$70 - $85**
1957 Girl with Umbrella	**$125 - $150**
1957 Luncheon	**$75 - $85**
1958 Picnic Basket (illus.)	**$15 - $25**
1960's Barefoot Boy (illus.)	**$40 - $50**
1960's Old Oaken Bucket (illus.)	**$40 - $50**
1961 Pansy Garden	**$15 - $20**
1969 Lillian Nordica (illus.)	**$30 - $35**
1972 Signed by Hamilton King	**$10 - $15**
1975 Lillian Russell (illus.)	**$10 - $15**
1975 Hilda Clark	**$10 - $15**
1981 Santa in Chair with Elves (illus.)	**$15 - $20**

Above, left:
1969. Lillian Nordica.
$30 - $35

Above, right:
1975. Lillian Russell.
$10 - $15

Below, right:
1981. Santa in Chair with Elves.
$15 - $20

Rare Glass Bottle

RARE GLASS BOTTLE
marked "E.S. Belton, London, Canada West,
This bottle never sold," and with a date of
1863. **$200**

Stone
Ginger Beers

The popularity of antique collecting has increased very rapidly in the last decade and the pace is accelerating. There are undoubtedly many complex reasons for this, one being the investment motive with the widespread belief that antiques and collectables are a relatively stable commodity. Generally speaking, collectables of first-rate quality, which good named ginger beer bottles are categorized as, have shown percentage gains in value over the last few years considerably greater than have mediocre or commonplace antiques.

Ginger beer, a beverage flavored with fermented ginger root, was a favorite drink in England at the beginning of the nineteenth century and later in America as a substitute for real beer. During prohibition ginger beer was one of the so-called temperence brews, although lightly fermented with an approximate 2 per cent alcoholic content. Because of its taste and the fact that it had a head, it was more a beer than a wine. This fashionable beverage of the day began to lose its popularity to other flavored drinks around the time of World War I (1914 – 1918).

**OLD HOMESTEAD
GINGER BEER BOTTLE,**
Manufactured by the International Drug Co. St. Stephen N.B. and Calais, Maine. **$45 - $80**

James Dyson Ginger Beer Bottle made by Bourne Denby, England **$20**

ATKINSON (a) $800 - $1000; (b) $300 - $400 (c) $300 - $400

William Atkinson was a beverage bottler of long standing in Guelph, operating from 1861 to 1899, taking over the business of Thomas Atkinson - first at part lot 110 Macdonell Street and later at 52 Liverpool Street. Impressed in the early hand-formed blob top bottle is "W. Atkinson, Guelph C.W." The blue stamping on the cream coloured bottle in the centre reads "W. Atkinson, Ginger Beer, Guelph, Ontario." The marking on the latest of the Atkinson bottles at the right says "W. Atkinson, Ginger Beer, Guelph." Impressed into the clay at the bottom of this later bottle is the name of the Scottish bottle manufacturer - H. Kennedy, Barrowfield Potteries, Glasgow.

The collecting of stone ginger beer bottles is a well established and growing hobby that is at the present time receiving a great deal of renewed interest. Among the many collectable bottles, those used by the Guelph bottlers are eagerly sought and treasured by collectors. In style and manufacture, the Guelph bottles are not unlike the type found throughout Ontario, but for some unknown reason, finding a Guelph ginger beer bottle of any name is difficult.

The early ginger beer bottles used in the 1850's and 1860's were hand formed with the name of the drink manufacturer often incised, as a lasting advertisement, into the pottery in the neck area. Because they were hand made, the capacity of the bottles varied from approximately nine ounces to 14 ounces. The closure of the primitive bottles was a cork held by a wire anchored around the blob top. The later machine-made pottery bottles had a label or design stamped with the brewer's name in black print, or sometimes blue, under the translucent glaze. Different methods were used to seal the contents of these bottles depending on the style of the bottle top. With the invention of

The oldest known of the Guelph ginger beer bottles are those used by George Beavis and James Copp. From 1857 to 1863 the Beavis and Copp partnership operated on Kent Street in the town of Guelph. Note the different markings. The name incised on the bottle at the left reads "BEAVIS & COPP GUELPH" and on the one on the right is "COPP & BEAVIS." (All bottles are from the Blyth collection).

BEAVIS & COPP
$500 - $700

COPP & BEAVIS
$600 - $800

the lightning stopper in 1875, the bottling industry had a new practical closure. The lightning stopper, used on collar top bottles, consisted of a wire bale holding secure a rubber ringed porcelain stopper. There were other variations on closure, but most utilized the basic principles of a rubber ringed stopper and some type of wire bale. The crown top, a cork-lined metal cap, patented in 1891, eventually made all other closures obsolete. This closure was essentially the same as those on beverage bottles today.

A great number of the ginger beer bottles used by Canadian manufacturers were ordered and shipped from pottery companies in England and Scotland. Ceramic industries there were well established to the point that American potters could not successfully compete. Pottery bottles were quite heavy and because of this characteristic they were popular with the masters of shipping vessels as ballast. Ships returning after delivering cargo to Europe often sailed with partially filled holds and so there was always an interest in shipments of heavy goods.

Manufacturers reused the stoneware bottles. These durable containers were seldom broken and survived many trips from the bottler to the consumer and back again. The pottery was thick, the bottles were heavy, and were most often delivered in wooden cases. The product was sold within a limited area through grocery stores, soda fountains, hotels, clubs and the like.

Why did some manufacturers refer to the beverage as stone ginger beer? Why was the drink contained in stoneware? Was it because stoneware was considered stronger than glass, or because stoneware kept the contents at a cooler more even temperature and shielded the ginger beer from the light? Perhaps pottery bottles had disadvantages also - they were difficult to fill by sight, it was difficult to determine how much substance remained in them

JAMES COPP (a) $600 - $800   (b) $600 - $800

Between 1859 and 1862 James Copp (of Beavis and Copp) had his own establishment at lot one on Woolwich Street. According to the 1861 census his annual production was 3000 gallons of ginger wine, etc. "James Copp, Guelph" is the wording impressed in his stoneware bottles. These bottles, although similar, have a two ounce capacity difference.

and it was difficult to insure their cleanliness for reuse. Unlike other stoneware utility vessels, which were phased out around the turn of the century with the rise of the glass industry, the use of stone ginger beer bottles continued until well into the 1920's. It was probably due to health standards that the pottery bottles were finally disposed of.

What made the collecting of these named artifacts so stimulating and rewarding is the fact that through a study of assessment rolls, census records, directories and period newspapers it is possible to find the location of the manufacturers and the date in which they operated. This allows the collector to more accurately pinpoint the origins of a particular piece which in turn can enhance its value.

Ginger beer and other pops were produced from 1901 to 1920 by George Kickley, Guelph Bottling Works. His first business was operated from 20 Powell Street and in 1917 he was listed as operating at 17 Robinson Avenue. It is believed that George Kickley also brewed ginger beer for John Thompson of Hamilton. Two variations of the Guelph Kickley bottles are known to exist. The very plain lettering on the bottle at the left reads "Brewed Ginger Beer, G. Kickley." Marked under the label is Munderloh and Co. Montreal, the maker of the bottle. The bottle at the right, referred to as the fancy Kickley, has the most elaborate design of any of the Guelph ginger beers and reads "Guelph Bottling Works, Ginger Beer, Geo. Kickley."

Left to right:
KICKLEY $150 - $200
KICKLEY $600 - $800

"Ye Olde English, Stone Ginger Beer, made by, James Ryder, Mineral Water Manufacturer, Guelph, Ontario. This bottle must be returned or paid for" is the inscription on the bottle used by James Ryder. Throughout his time in operation, 1910 to 1937, Ryder manufactured drinks at a number of different locations in Guelph. From his first location at 104 Dublin Street he moved to 14 London Road, then to Masonic Temple building on Quebec Street, on to 58 Clinton Street and finally at 175 Queen Street.

RYDER $200 - $300

In 1908 Albert Reinhart purchased the Reed Brothers beverage business and continued until 1971 to manufacture drinks. "Royal City Mineral Water Works. A. Reinhart, Guelph" is the wording in a circle around the Reinhart logo. Kennedy of Glasgow was also the maker of the Reinhart bottle. To clarify the confusion of the addresses of the three related industries operating from the same location we might add that the street name was changed at different times throughout the years, starting with Matthews at Brock Road, Reed at Dundas Road and finally Reinhart at Gordon Street.

REINHART
$200 - $300

Left to right: **MATTHEWS $500 - $600,   MATTHEWS $300 - $400**
MATTHEWS $300 - $500

From 1873 to 1906 Alex Matthews manufactured ginger beer and carbonated beverages at 247 Brock Road in Guelph. Shown here are three different styles of bottles used during his time in business. The two on the right were produced by the Kennedy potters of Glasgow.

GINGER BEER – Take 20 oz. of ground ginger. Take 20 gals. of boiling water, put the water on the ginger in lots of 5 gals. till strength is all out. Then take this liquid and add 2 ozs. cream tartar, 2 ozs. tartaric acid, let stand 12 hours, draw off and then add 20 lbs. sugar 2 ozs. lemon extract 1 ozs. cream. Foam in 2 ozs. brewers yeast. Let stand 24 hours, draw off and bottle.

A ginger beer recipe found in a book previously belonging to the Reinhart family in Guelph.

Left::
Reed Brothers took over the Alex Matthews bottling works in 1906. A short two years later, in 1908, the business was dissolved. The Reed ginger beer bottle is different to the others in that the labelling is printed in blue and reads "Reed Bros. Stone Ginger Beer, Works Dundas Road, Guelph. This Bottle must be returned when empty."
REED $400 - $600

This data regarding Guelph Ginger Beer Bottles was originally gathered by Mrs Don Blyth and Scott Jordan for Antique Showcase magazine, and has now been updated.

Gurd's, Montreal, Que. **Each $45**

O'Keefe's Advertising Sign.
Amber, black and yellow.
Ca. 1940's. **$85**

O'Keefe's   Each $40

Left to right:
Milloy, Montreal, Que.
$105

Milloy, Montreal, Que.
$90,

Milloy, Montreal, Que.
$105

Left to right:
Fortier, Quebec, Que.   **$90**
Fortier, Quebec, Que.   **$70**

Above left to right:
Allan's, Montreal, Que.   **$50**
Nutter, Montreal, Que.   **$80**

Below left to right:
Christin & Cie, Montreal, Que.   **$85**
Christin & Cie, Montreal, Que.   **$100**

Left to right:
Perry, Kingston, Ont.
(cracked) **$200**

Thompson, Kingston, Ont. **$150**

Thompson, Hamilton, Ont. **$70**

Left to right:
Pilgrim Bros., Hamilton, Ont.
$85

Cummer & Co., Hamilton, Ont.
$65

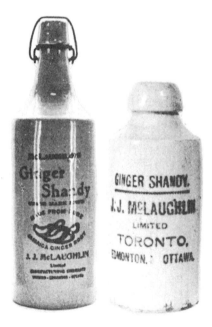

Left to right:
McLaughlin, Toronto, Ont.
$85

McLaughlin, Toronto, Edmonton,
Ottawa **$165**

Left to right:
Drolet & Co., Ottawa, Ont.
$250

Charles Wilson, Toronto, Ont.
$100

Left to right:
Atlantic, Halifax, N.S. **$65**
Indian Beer, Halifax, N.S. **$100**
Dixon, Halifax, N.S. **$55**

Left to right:
Quinn, Halifax, N.S. **$65**
Quinn, Halifax, N.S. **$70**

Left to right:
Roue, Halifax, N.S. **$80**
Roue, Halifax, N.S. **$100**

Left to right:
Roue, Halifax, N.S. **$105**
Roue, Halifax, N.S. **$55**

Left to right:
Terris, St. John, N.B. **$80**
Terris, St. John, N.B. **$135**
Terris, St. John, N.B. **$80**

Left to right:
Old Homestead, St. Stephen, N.B. & Calais, Maine **$50**
Old Homestead, St. Stephen, N.B. & Calais, Maine **$80**

Left to right:
Dolan Bros., St. John, N.B. **$100**
Sussex Mineral Spring Co. **$70**

Left to right:
Simmons, Charlottetown **$225**
Bennett, St. John's Nfld. **$135**

Left to right:

Drewry, Winnipeg, Man. $155

Kings, Winnipeg, Man. $80

Brandon Brewing $135

Left to right:

Empire Brewing, Brandon, Man.
$130

Empire Brewing, Brandon, Man.
$150

Left to right:

Saskatoon Bottling Works
$145

Empire Brewing, Brandon, Man.
$165

Left to right:

Kings, Winnipeg & Saskatoon
$80

Crystal Spring, Moose Jaw, Sask.
$135

Left to right:
Phillips, Calgary, Alberta **$100**
Phillips, Calgary, Alberta **$90**

Left to right:
Thorpes, Vancouver, B.C. **$80**
Thorpes, Vancouver, B.C. **$105**

Left to right:
Kirk & Co., Victoria, B.C. **$70**
Old English Beverage Co.,
Victoria, B.C. **$135**
Regal, Victoria, B.C. **$65**

**Country Club
Beverage Co. Ltd.,**
$80

THE "LIGHTNING"
BOTTLE STOPPER

Patented Jan. 5, 1875. Re-issued June 5, 1877.

Trade Mark, "Lightning," Registered Feb. 12, 1876.

MANUFACTURED ONLY BY
HENRY W. PUTNAM.

HE "LIGHTNING" STOPPER has been for several years successfully used in the business of bottling Ale, Beer and Cider. Several of the largest Bottlers in this country who steam their beer are using this Stopper instead of corks.

The "LIGHTNING" STOPPERS are also being largely used upon Beer Bottles for export by parties who report that their sales of Beer have been greatly increased, particularly in California and Texas, by reason of the ready market for Beer bottled with the "LIGHTNING" STOPPER attached.

Having Secured the Exclusive Right for the United States and Dominion of Canada to manufacture and sell the Patent

"Lightning" Bottle Stopper

I am prepared to furnish it in quantities to suit purchasers.

Price, $5.00 Per Gross.

As much depends upon a correct adjustment of the Stopper, it is essential that a Sample Bottle be sent with orders.

Rubber Tubing for Filling Beer Bottles, 12-Feet Lengths-----Each $1.00.

TERMS---NET CASH.-------Payable in New York Par Funds.

Having made arrangements with nearly all the Glass Manufacturers of the United States and Canada to sell the

"LIGHTNING" BOTTLE STOPPER

Bottlers can buy their Bottles of the Glass Manufacturers, with the "Lightning" Stoppers attached, ready for Use.

I am aware that parties are offering for sale Bottle Stoppers that are a direct infringement upon the rights secured to me under several of the large number of Patents which I now own, and most respectfully advise all persons to examine into the matter thoroughly before buying, using or dealing in Bottle Stoppers, or any PART or PARTS THEREOF, not manufactured by me, as I shall hold all parties responsible who use or deal in Bottle Stoppers which infringe upon rights secured to me by Letters Patent.

ALL ORDERS WILL RECEIVE PROMPT ATTENTION.

Samples Sent and Further Information Promptly Given Upon Application.

HENRY W. PUTNAM
108 Chambers Street, New York City.

An advertisement taken from The Western Brewer and Journal of the Barley, Malt and Hop Trades · Vol. XV No. 1, Chicago, New York, Jan. 15, 1890.

Syphon Bottles

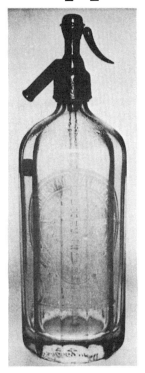

Above, left to right:

"GURD'S OF MONTREAL"
Clear,acid etched label. Ht. 12 3/4". **$25**

"DOMINION DRY GINGER ALE CO., TORONTO"
Clear 12 3/4". **$25**

"DOMINION SODA WATER M.F.G., TORONTO, ONT."
Clear. **$25**

SIPHONS

Many soda siphons found in Canada appear to have been made in England. The British Siphon Co. of London was one of the largest manufacturers.

Left:

"TORONTO STONE GINGER BEER CO."
by the The British Siphon Co., London.
Pale green. Ht. 13 1/2". **$200-300**

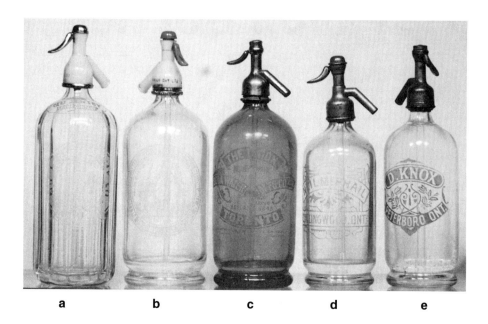

a   b   c   d   e

Left to right:

a) "JERSEY CREME CO TORONTO."
Clear with a logo of an "elephant." Matching plastic and metal top, and ground base. Minor internal and external flaws. 13" tall. **$15**

b) "J CHRISTIN & CO/ MONTREAL."
Circular etching containing a logo of a dog touching the syphon which causes it to spray a cat. Clear bottle with ground base. Plastic top marked "DOMINION DRY LTD/TORONTO." Minor internal haze, some light external scratches, 1 tiny chip to base and 1 light bruise to base. **$53**

c) "THE UNION/SODA WATER MFG CO/TORONTO."
Blue with an "OKEEFE" metal top. Ground base. Minor external scratches and some very light internal haze/water spots. **$75**

d) "MCPHAIL/COLLINGWOOD ONT."
Clear with the name surrounded by banners. "TORONTO SODA WATER CO" metal top. A coup of external tiny surface nicks. Internal has the usual light water spots. Smaller than normal size. 3 5/8" x 11 1/2". **$43**

e) "D KNOX/PETERBORO ONT."
Clear with name in dark banners and surrounded by flora pattern. Matching metal stopper shows signs of wear. Minor internal and external scratches. 3 3/8" x 11 3/4". **$75**

a   b   c   d   e

Left to right:

a) "EMPRESS/EMPIRE BREWING CO/BRANDON MAN."
Clear bottle with ground base and a "POMEROY BOTTLING WORKS," metal top. Has 1 1/4" bruise to edge and base. Light overall internal haze/water spots. **$15**

b) "CREDIT VALLEY/BOTTLING/ WORKS/GLEN WILLIAMS/ ONTARIO."
Clear bottle with a ground base and matching metal top. This syphon is considered scarce or even rare. Usual internal haze and 1 tiny ping to face of bottle. **$68**

c) "PLAZA BEVERAGE/ 25¢ DEPOSIT/NY."
Clear bottle with ground base and metal top marked, "A ROSENBERG NY 59." 2 pings to face and some light internal haze. **$20**

d) "J D BROWN/GRAVEN- HURST ONT."
Clear bottle with lettering within a darker shield and has a logo of a bottling machine. "BRITISH SYPHON" metal top. Couple of tiny pings to face of bottle and the usual internal haze. **$65**

e) "J DODDS/SODA WATER WORKS C4th" (in logo of a Diamond.)
Main lettering is surrounded with a floral pattern. Clear bottle with a ground lip and a "PUNCH DRY MFG CO/TORONTO" metal top. 1/2" long chip from base at edge. Usual internal haze. **$45**

Methods of Bottle Making

No one knows for sure where or when glass was first manufactured. Drawings on ancient tombs in Egypt depict workmen who are free blowing vessels using methods common until the middle of the nineteenth century.

Glassmaking is a relatively young industry in Canada. Most bottles used by Canadian bottlers prior to 1865 were imported from Europe and the United States. The industry expanded with the growth of population and glass factories were established across Canada to supply the demand for glass containers.

Sand, the common ingredient in all glass, melted with soda or potash and lime, was used to make bottle glass. The batch was placed in melting pots inside a furnace and heated to temperatures ranging from 2,200 degrees to 2,700 degrees Fahrenheit. Cullet, clean pieces of broken glass, was added to the raw materials to speed up the melting process. It took several hours for the ingredients to melt, fuse and form a liquid known as the metal.

Prior to the invention of the automatic bottle machine, bottle manufacturing was very labour intensive, requiring a team of workers to make a single bottle. For either free blown or blown in the mold bottles each crew consisted of three to seven men. A skilled glass blower, the head man or gaffer, was assisted by a workman who gathered the metal on the blowpipe. Other assistants and apprentices worked with the team as the shaping of a bottle progressed.

Free Blown

A workman, known as the gatherer, would dip the blowpipe into the molten glass through an opening in the furnace called the bocca. Twisting the pipe he would gather the metal on to the end of it and when he had the required amount of molten glass on the pipe he would carry it over to the marver, a flat stone or metal surface, where he would roll the gob of glass back and forth to shape it. With a few puffs of air through the blowpipe he would expand the glass slightly. Then the pipe was swung or spun to further shape the molten glass. At this point the gaffer took over. Sitting on a bench with arms to support the blowpipe, he would roll the pipe on the arm of the "chair" to maintain the shape of the inflated gather (the parison), at the same time forming the neck of the bottle using a tool known as a jack. After more heating, turning, and blowing the bubble assumed a definite shape. A pontil rod was attached to the base to hold the bottle while the gaffer removed it from the blowpipe and shaped the lip. He then removed the rod and the apprentice took the bottle to the annealing oven. The final step of annealing consisted of gradual cooling, since cooling quickly from a high temperature causes glass to explode. Each bottle was placed in the lehr, a chamber through which all bottles must pass while the temperature slowly decreases to about 70 degrees Fahrenheit.

Bottles shaped by blowing and manipulation have no seam marks. Early free blown bottles have a circular pontil scar on the base, which was left jagged and unfinished on utilitarian bottles but ground off on the more expensive and decorative types. About 1850 the snap case was invented; a mechanical device which held the base of the bottle in a small cup with two arms to grip the bottle at the shoulder and hold it in place for finishing. Bottles held by a snap case do not have a pontil scar on the base.

Mold Blown (1800-1920)

These bottles are blown with the aid of a mold. The gaffer, using a blowpipe with a parison at one end, shaped a bottle by blowing into the pipe until the glass assumed the shape of the mold. The mold was then opened by an apprentice and the bottle still on the blowpipe was removed to have an empontilling rod attached or to be held in a snap case while the gaffer removed the blowpipe. To do this a mark was made around the neck with a cold wet wooden paddle, then a sharp tap on the neck would free the bottle from the blowpipe at the desired spot. The neck of the nearly completed bottle was reheated in a small furnace and a lipping tool was used to apply the desired type of lip. The finished product was then placed in the lehr to cool gradually.

Mold seams are of interest to collectors because they tell how a bottle was formed. Molds made of cast iron in two or more pieces were hinged to open and close. Each junction point of the parts of the mold left a surface mark on a container blown in the mold.

Dating bottles by using the method of manufacture as a guide is sometimes difficult. Modernization progressed haltingly and manufacturing techniques that were discontinued in one factory often remained in use at others.

(1800 - 1840) DIP MOLD
A tapered one piece mold used to form the body of a bottle, the shoulder and neck being hand finished. A bottle blown in a Dip Mold has a uniformly shaped body, often with a seam mark visible just below the shoulder.

(1810 - 1890) TWO-PIECE MOLD – A mold hinged to open at the base. Bottles blown in a Two-Piece Mold have a continuous seam across the bottom and up both sides to the lip.

(1870 - 1900) POST-BOTTOM MOLD – Bottles blown in a Post Bottom Mold have a circular seam in the centre of the base, the mold mark continuing from the central seam up the body and neck of the bottle.

(1870 - 1910) THREE-PIECE DIP MOLD – An integrated mold consisting of a Dip Mold base to form the body and a two-piece hinged top to form the shoulder and neck. Seams are visible just below the shoulder and up the neck of the bottle.

(1880 - 1910) TURN MOLD A term used to describe a bottle that was spun in the mold after blowing to obliterate seam marks. Usually faint scoring can be seen round the circumference of bottles turned in a mold.

A mold seam mark that does not continue over the lip of a bottle is an indication that a bottle was blown in a mold. This is because the tool used to shape the lip would erase part of the mold seam mark on the neck. Some mold blown bottles do have a seam mark through the lip. These were blown in a BLOW-BACK MOLD (1850 - ?)

AUTOMATIC BOTTLE MACHINE

The fully automatic bottle machine invented in the United States by Michael Owens at the beginning of the twentieth century changed the glass industry dramatically, and by 1906 automatic machines were being used in Canadian glass factories to produce bottles. Each bottle

Hand Operated Lipping Tool

which was a type of mold with a bubble-like extension above a threaded lip cut into the mold. The bubble above the mold-formed lip was severed by the glass blower after the bottle had been formed.

Many mold blown bottles are found with embossed lettering or symbols. Molds had words and/or logos engraved or stamped into them, such as the product name, product manufacturer's name and address, instructions and the weight or liquid measure of the contents. Another method of embossing was to insert lettered plates into a blank mold making custom made bottles available at a lower cost. Patent dates and the glass factory's trade mark were often embossed on the base of bottles.

delivered automatically from the machine was standardized making it possible for glass factories to mass produce bottles to satisfy the ever increasing demand.

Mold seam marks on the automatic machine made bottles continue up through the lip to the top of the bottle.

Automatic Bottle Machine.

The Colour of Glass

"Green glass" is a glassmaker's term which describes the colour of the metal used to make bottles. It is the trace elements of iron found in sand, the world over, that produces the natural greenish-blue colour of glass. Because the amount of iron present in sand varies at each geographic location early bottles are found in many shades of blues and greens i.e. bluish-green, greenish-blue, turquoise, and aquamarine.

In the late 1800's consumer demand for clear bottles and containers caused glass manufacturers to add manganese oxide to the raw materials. This chemical when added to the batch rendered glass colourless and the use of this oxide continued until about 1915. Glass made with manganeses added for the purpose of clarity, will turn amethyst when exposed to the ultra-violet rays of the sun for an extended period. From 1916 to 1930 selemium oxide was used to de-colourize the batch; this type of glass turns pale yellow after exposure to sunlight. The foregoing colours are described as being suncast amethyst or suncast yellow. After 1930 arsenic was used by glass manufacturers to produce clear glass containers.

In the production of coloured glass, specific shades were obtained by the addition of oxides in varying amounts.

BLACK	iron slag
BLUE	cobalt or copper
BROWN	carbon or nickel
GREEN	chronium, copper or iron
OPAQUE WHITE	tin or zinc
PINK	selenium
PURPLE	nickel or manganese
RED	copper, selenium or gold
YELLOW	iron or selenium

Lips and Closures

The earliest closure which bottle collectors are concerned with is the cork which was used over the longest period of time as a means to seal a bottle. Below are some of the types of lip finishes on bottles which were used to hold corks.

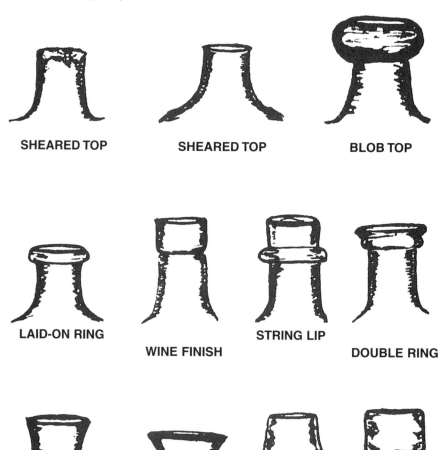

SHEARED TOP   SHEARED TOP   BLOB TOP

LAID-ON RING   WINE FINISH   STRING LIP   DOUBLE RING

FLARE   FUNNELLED   CASTOR OIL   CORK

**WIRED
CORK**

CORKS

Corks were the most often used bottle closures until the late 1800's. On beverage bottles such as beer and wine they were tied or wired down to prevent them from popping, wax or pitch was used as a sealant, if needed, on other types of bottles.

**WIRE CORK
FASTENER**

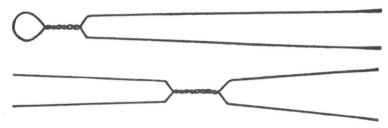

Two wire twists for securing corks -
Above: **GINGER ALE LOOP**
Below: **CENTRE TWIST LOOP**

During the late 1800's many new types of bottle closures were invented. Because an effective leak proof seal was important the neck and lip of bottles were re-designed to incorporate the different styles of closure.

GRAVITATING STOPPER

This closure, which was reusable by the bottler, was invented by John Matthews of New York in 1864. A glass rod with a rubber seal on one end was held in place on the neck of the bottle by the gas pressure of a carbonated beverage. To open, this closure was pushed down into the bottle releasing the internal pressure.

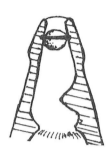

CODD'S BALL STOPPER

Another type of closure which could be reused by the bottler. Patented, 1872 by Hiram Codd in England. A variation of this design was patented in Canada in 1876. A glass ball was held in place by the gas in the soda against a rubber ring inside the lip of the bottle. To open the bottle the ball was pushed down, but was prevented from falling back into the lip or down into the body of the bottle by constrictions in the neck.

THREE TYPES OF LIGHTNING STOPPERS

LIGHTNING STOPPER

Invented by Charles de Quillfeldt of New York in 1875. Ale and ginger beer bottles as well as fruit jars were sealed by this method. This ingenious reusable closure was made of bent wire and a stopper. Refinements were made over the years, however, it was finally replaced early in the 20th century by the less expensive and more reliable devices.

HUTCHINSON'S PATENT SPRING SODA BOTTLE STOPPER

In 1879 Charles G. Hutchinson of Chicago invented this closure. The stopper, a loop of heavy wire with a gasket of rubber attached was reusable by the bottler. When the bottle had been filled the wire loop was pulled up and the gas from the carbonation in the soda sealed the bottle by pressing the rubber gasket firmly against the inside of the shoulder.

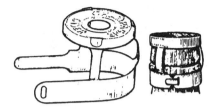

BERNARDIN METAL CAP WITH NECKBAND
An improved method of securing corks, invented by Alfred J. Bernardin of Evansville, Indiana sometime during the 1880's. This strip metal was used to fasten a metal disk over a cork to hold it in place.

BALTIMORE LOOP SEAL
A single use closure invented by William Painter of Baltimore, patented in 1885. Internal pressure held this closure in place. The metal loop on the rubber gasket was used to pry the closure from the lip of the bottle. Mr. Painter, a machinist, also invented a filling and sealing machine for bottlers and supplied bottle makers with tools to form the reverse taper required in the neck of bottles to be sealed with the Baltimore Loop.

INSIDE THREAD
Not a very popular method of sealing bottles. Used intermittently between 1860 and 1910 by bottlers of spirits and ginger beer.

GLASS & CORK STOPPER
The glass stopper fitted a cork liner in the neck of the bottle. This had the advantage of the bottle being able to be reclosed after use. Mainly for spirits and sauces.

CROWN CAP

The best of all closures, the Crown Cap was patented in 1891 by William Painter of Baltimore. Over the years it has become the universal stopper for beer and carbonated beverages. Bottles required a special lip and a capping tool was used to fit and seal the crimped metal cap. Although it was used on blown in the mold bottles the Crown Cap came into universal use soon after the invention of the automatic bottle making machine.

CONTINUOUS THREAD FINISH

John L. Mason patented his design for fruit jars with a threaded lip in 1858. Fruit jars of this type were sealed with a metal screw band and a glass lid. Many variations and improvements of his design followed. Screw caps became widely used on bottles after 1919 when the Continuous Thread Finish for bottle lips was patented. This invention which led to standardization and economical mass production was beneficial to both bottle manufacturers and packers.

KORK-N-SEAL

A resealable closure used mostly on liquor bottles during the 1920's and 30's. The twisted wire lever was flipped up to open the bottle and down to reseal it.

Factories

From about 1840 onwards glass containers for household and commercial use were manufactured in Canada. Prior to that time items of this type were imported into Canada from Europe and the United States.

Methods of manufacture gradually improved during the late 19th century and with the new technology the factories of Canada were able to satisfy the growing demand for large and small glass containers. During this period the industry was in a state of flux and by the end of the century seven factories had been absorbed by the blossoming Diamond Glass Company Limited which later became the Diamond Flint Glass Company Limited and in 1913 the Dominion Glass Company Limited. The output of the several plants of this large company, now known as Domglas Inc., still includes large quantities of bottles and jars for commercial and domestic use.

Canadian glass works, their dates of operation and the types of containers produced follows:

NOVA SCOTIA

THE HUMPHREYS GLASS COMPANY, Trenton-New Glasgow (1890 - 1917)
Bottles – (inks, medicinals, mucilage, sodas, whiskey flasks) and Fruit Jars.

THE LAMONT GLASS COMPANY, Trenton-New Glasgow (1890 - 1902)
Bottles – (inks, medicinals, sodas, whiskey flasks) and Fruit Jars. Items have been found marked as follows: "L G Co."

NEW BRUNSWICK

THE NEW BRUNSWICK CRYSTAL GLASS COMPANY, Saint John (1874 - 1878) The exact nature of the products of this factory is unknown at this time, however, it is believed that bottles and fruit jars were two of the items made there.

THE HUMPHREYS GLASS COMPANY, Moncton (1971 - 1920) Gerald Stevens in "Canadian Glass" states production appears to be the same as that of the Nova Scotia plant.

QUEBEC

FOSTER BROTHERS, St. Johns (1854 - 1860) Advertised that they made a variety of containers including beer and ginger beer bottles, pickle and candy jars, fruit jars, wines, inks, flasks, snuffs, vials and medicine bottles. To date the only type of bottle identified as a product of this factory is a torpedo bottle embossed "Foster Brothers St. Johns C.E."

OTTAWA GLASS WORKS, Como (1848 - 1857) became the BRITISH AMERICAN GLASS WORKS, Como (1857 - 1865) Exploration of the site has revealed that case gins and druggists' bottles were made there. It is also reported that soda water bottles were a product of these factories.

THE CANADA GLASS WORKS, Hudson (1867 - 1871) Advertised that they made several types of food and medicine bottles as well as fruit jars.

THE ST. LAWRENCE GLASS COMPANY, Montreal (1867 - 1873) S.J. Lyman, a member of the Lyman Sons & Co. drug firm in Montreal, was associated with the St. Lawrence Glass Company and was honoured at the opening ceremonies, Oct., 1867, as being the originator of the company. An exploration of the site revealed that bottles were made at the St. Lawrence Glass Company and a blue "Lyman Sons & Co. Citrate Magnesia" bottle was found. Items have been found marked as follows: "ST L."

THE (EARLY) DOMINION GLASS COMPANY, Montreal (1886 - 1898) Fruit jars embossed with the word "Dominion" in an arc have been attributed to this factory.

THE ST. JOHNS GLASS COMPANY, St. Johns (1875 - 1878) was purchased by William Yuille and became **THE EXCELSIOR GLASS COMPANY** (1879 - 1880) Examples of products from these firms have not been identified, but it is reported that they made mould blown containers.

In 1880 **THE EXCELSIOR GLASS COMPANY** moved to Montreal and operated under that name until 1883. The following series of factory names reflect the changes of ownership and reorganization that took place over three decades.
North American Glass Company Limited (1883 - 1890)

Diamond Glass Company Limited (1890 - 1902)

Diamond Flint Glass Company Limited (1903 - 1913)

Dominion Glass Company Limited (1913 - 1925)

Containers in a variety of types and forms were made over the years at the Delormier Avenue site of these factories. A general list would include - Bottles -

(bitters/druggists'/medicinals, cosmetics, ketchups, limes, milks, mineral waters, pickles, pops, perfumes, sodas, waters, whiskey flasks), Candy Jars, Fruit Jars, and Packers. The trademark of the Dominion Glass Company Limited is a "D" in a diamond.

CONSUMERS GLASS COMPANY LIMITED,

Montreal (1913 - present) Bottles - (beer, milk, prescription, soda) and Fruit Jars. A "C" in a triangle has been the trademark of this company since 1917 and was used until 1961 when it was changed to a "C" in a triangle with rounded corners.

Consumers Glass Company Limited manufacturers containers in Canada with plants at - Candiac and Ville Ste. Pierre, Quebec; Milton and Toronto, Ontario; and Lavington, British Columbia.

ONTARIO

MALLORYTOWN GLASS WORKS, Mallorytown (1839 -
1840) A whiskey flask and bottle are illustrated by Gerald Stevens in "Early Canadian Glass" as products of this factory.

THE CALEDONIA GLASS WORKS, Caledonia (1844-ca.
1848) Produced bottles and bottled the natural mineral waters on the site of the springs near Prescott, Ontario. To date no examples have been identified.

THE HAMILTON GLASS WORKS, Hamilton (1865 -
1898) Re-opened 1906. Bottles – (horseradish, pickle, pop, soda, soda water) and Fruit Jars. Items have been found marked as follows: "Hamilton," "Hamilton Glass Works," and "HGW." Items marked "Rutherford & Co." were produced during George Rutherford's ownership of the Hamilton Glass Works (1872 - 1893).

THE BURLINGTON GLASS WORKS, Hamilton
(1874 - 1897) It is believed that many types of bottles were made at this factory and it is known that ink and mucilage bottles were produced there as well as fruit jars. Items have been found marked as follows: "Burlington," "BGW," and "BGCo."

THE NAPANEE GLASS WORKS, Napanee (1881 -
1883) Shards of druggists' bottles have been found on the factory site.

THE ERIE GLASS WORKS,
Port Colborne (1893 - 1898) Bottles - (ales, inks, whiskeys) and Fruit Jars. Items have been found marked on the base as follows: "ERIE" and "E" in a hexagon.

THE TORONTO GLASS COMPANY, Toronto (1893 -
1920) Bottles – (flasks, inks,

The Sydenham Glass Company, Wallaceburg

medicinals) and Fruit Jars. Items have been found marked as follows "TGCo."

THE SYDENHAM GLASS COMPANY, Wallaceburg (1894 - 1913) Bottles – (ink, pickle) and Fruit Jars.

THE FOSTER GLASS WORKS, Port Colborne (1895 - 1899) Believed to have produced fruit jars, but no examples have been identified to date.

THE BEAVER FLINT GLASS COMPANY, Toronto (1897 - 1948) This factory advertised that they sold containers and it is now believed that they were distributors only and not container manufacturers. Medicinals with the mark "B F G Co." on the base usually have a small "D" in a diamond mark as well indicating that the Dominion Glass Company manufactured some bottles for this firm.

THE ONTARIO GLASS WORKS, Kingsville (1899 - 1902) The "Ferrol" cod liver oil bottle and "Beaver" fruit jars are attributed to this factory. The Ontario Glass Works advertised in a local newspaper regarding the "Monarch" fruit jar, but to date an example of this jar has not been found.

RICHARDS GLASS COMPANY, Toronto (established 1912) Prescription bottles ("Queen Oval" - "King Oval" - "Princess"), vials and nursers marked "Rigo" or "R G Co. T" were distributed by this firm, but made by the Dominion Glass Company.

THE JEFFERSON GLASS COMPANY, Toronto (1913 - 1925) Certain types of "Crown" fruit jars have been attributed to this factory.

See "A Collectors Manual Fruit Jars" by Julian H. Toulouse.

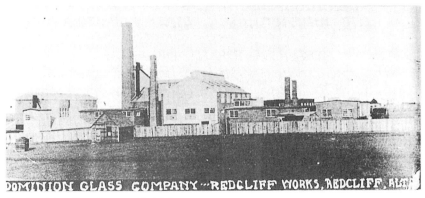

The Dominion Glass Company, Redcliff

MANITOBA

THE MANITOBA GLASS MANUFACTURING COMPANY, Beausejour (1904 - 1913) Bottle – (beer, druggist, ink, milk, pop, prescription, soda, spirit) and Fruit Jars. Items have been found marked as follows: "B" on base.

MID-WEST GLASS COMPANY, Winnipeg, (1929 - 1937) Bottles – (milk, prescription, soda) Fruit Jars and Packers. Items have been found marked as follows: "M" in a circle.

ALBERTA

THE DOMINION GLASS COMPANY, Redcliff (1913 - present) Bottles – (beer, medicinal, mineral water) and Fruit Jars.

BRITISH COLUMBIA

THE CRYSTAL GLASS COMPANY, Sapperton (now New Westminster) (1907 - 1908) Bottles – (all kinds including beer, milk, pickle, prescription) and Fruit Jars.

THE VICTORIA GLASS & BOTTLE COMPANY, Victoria (1913 - 1916) Little is known about this company which was in business for only about three years, therefore, their production, if any, would have been rather small. John Barclay in "The Canadian Fruit Jar Report" mentions a report in which it states the factory would make all the various sizes of bottles and jars for firms in Victoria and Vancouver as well as the Hudson Bay Company. No examples of this firm's products have been identified at this time.

THE DEVELOPMENT AND STRUCTURE OF THE DOMINION GLASS COMPANY LIMITED

The DIAMOND GLASS COMPANY LIMITED was formed in 1890 and acquired control of the following glass factories in Canada throughout the period of its incorporation which ended in 1903.

1890 - The Burlington Glass Works, Hamilton, Ontario
North American Glass Works, Montreal, Quebec
Nova Scotia Glass Company, Trenton-New Glasgow, N.S.
1893 - The Hamilton Glass Works, Hamilton, Ontario
1897 - The Toronto Glass Company, Toronto, Ontario
1898 - The (Early) Dominion Glass Company, Montreal, Que.
The Lamont Glass Company, Trenton-New Glasgow, N.S.

The DIAMOND GLASS COMPANY LIMITED was reorganized in 1903 and the name was changed to the DIAMOND FLINT GLASS COMPANY LIMITED and during the period 1903 to 1913 gained control of two other independent glass companies.

1907 - The Manitoba Glass Manufacturing Company, Beausejour, Manitoba
1908 - The Sydenham Glass Company, Wallaceburg, Ontario.

In 1906 the Hamilton Glass Works factory was re-opened and a new factory, the Canadian Glass Manufacturing Company Limited, was built in 1907 at Pte. St. Charles, Quebec.
Reorganization took place again in 1913 when the company became the DOMINION GLASS COMPANY LIMITED and expansion continued with the acquisition of the Jefferson Glass Company, Toronto, Ontario. Also in 1913 the company opened a factory at Redcliff, Alberta.

The company, now known as Domglas Inc., manufacturers glass containers in Canada with plants at -
Moncton and Scoudouc, New Brunswick; Montreal, Quebec; Mississauga, Ontario; Redcliff, Alberta; and Burnaby, British Columbia.

Containers are also currently being produced at the Libbey-St Clair Inc. factory, Wallaceburg, Ontario. For the last 90 years, glass items have been manufactured at this site. Libbey-St Clair Inc. is jointly owned by Domglas Inc. of Canada and the Libbey Division of Owens-Illinois, U.S.A.

Glass Makers Marks

Marks used by Canadian glass factories are illustrated below. Occasionally wholesalers had their trade mark embossed on bottles. Although they sometimes designed their own bottles they did not actually make them. Due to the many changes of ownership and amalgamations that took place in the late 1800's and early in this century it is not always possible to date a container by the manufacturer's mark.

Information regarding Canadian factories and jobbers may be found in the preceding section – "Factories."

BEAVER FLINT GLASS COMPANY

B F G Co.

NOTE: Containers marked "B F G Co" were probably made by the Dominion Glass Company and its predecessors.

BURLINGTON GLASS WORKS

B G W

1875 - 1877

BURLINGTON

1875 - 1897

BG Co

1877 - 1897

CONSUMERS GLASS COMPANY LIMITED

1917 - 1961   1961 -

Possibly the DIAMOND GLASS COMPANY LIMITED Or the (EARLY) DOMINION GLASS COMPANY

D G Co

NOTE: A shard from a fruit jar embossed "D G Co" in a maple leaf was found at the Burlington Glass Works site. It seems likely that jars marked in this way were made at Burlington during the period of the Diamond Glass Company's ownership.

(EARLY) DOMINION GLASS COMPANY

1886 - 1898

DOMINION GLASS COMPANY LIMITED

1913 -

ERIE GLASS WORKS

E (in hexagon)

1893 - 1898

ERIE

EXCELSIOR GLASS COMPANY LIMITED

E G Co

1879 - 1883

1879 - 1883

EXCELSIOR

1879 - 1883

EXCELSIOR IMPROVED

1879 - 1883

NOTE: This type of mark is found on fruit jar lids which are also embossed with the company name.

NOTE: This type of mark is found on fruit jar lids which are also embossed with the company name.
A baby feeder ("Excelsior Feeder") is also embossed with this mark.

HAMILTON GLASS WORKS

HAMILTON

1865 - 1872

1865 - 1895

HAMILTON GLASS WORKS

1865 - 1872

NOTE: This mark is found on the base of some "Greek Key Safety Valve" fruit jars

RUTHERFORD & Co.

1872 - 1893

NOTE: Used on fruit jars during George Rutherford's ownership of the Hamilton Glass Works.

 HGW

Ca. 1893 - 1898
& 1906 -

LAMONT GLASS COMPANY

 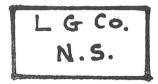

1890 - 1899

MANITOBA GLASS MANUFACTURING CO.

B

MIDWEST GLASS COMPANY

RICHARDS GLASS COMPANY

RIGO

NOTE: This company designed several types of prescription bottles and baby feeders. Although their trade mark often appears on bottles, the Richards Glass Company was a wholesaler and not a manufacturer.

ST. LAWRENCE GLASS COMPANY

STL

TORONTO GLASS COMPANY

T.G.C°

Glossary

ABM

Refers to bottles made by automatic bottle machine.

APPLIED COLOURED LABELS (ACL)

A labelling process developed in the United States during the 1920's which came into popular use during the 1930's on milk and soft drink bottles.

A paste made of borasilicate, oil and a colouring oxide was applied to bottles through a steel screen. The labelled bottle then had to be baked at a temperature of about 300 degrees Fahrenheit. If the label consisted of two colours the first colour applied had to dry before the next one could be added. A slow and expensive process.

In the 1940's it was discovered that by using a plastic resin in place of the oil in the mixture, drying time between applications of colour was almost eliminated, thus speeding the process and making it more common procedure.

APPLIED LIP

The lip of a bottle shaped by the use of a hand held lipping tool.

BIM

Refers to bottles blown in the mold.

BIMAL

Refers to bottles blown in the mold with an applied lip.

DEBOSSED

The impressed lettering or logo on pottery bottles.

EMBOSSED

Raised letters and/or trade mark on mold blown or machine made bottles or jars.

FIRE POLISHED

Finished glass containers reheated to smooth the finish and obliterate seams and tool marks.

FREE BLOWN

Bottles blown and shaped by manipulation without the aid of a mold.

GROUND LIP

Early blown in the mold fruit jars had the lip ground to make a good sealing surface. Automatic bottle machine jars have smooth lips.

HAND BLOWN

See mold blown.

LAID-ON-RING (LIP)

The addition of a strip of glass to the neck of a bottle to form a lip
– Not uniform in appearance.

MOLD BLOWN

Bottles blown by a glassblower and shaped with the aid of a mold.

PONTIL MARK

Scar on the base of free blown or mold blown bottles where pontil rod was attached. Some pontil marks are jagged and unfinished, others have been smoothed by grinding.

PONTIL ROD

A metal rod which was attached to the base of a free blown or mold blown bottle to hold it in place while the gaffer removed the bottle from the blowpipe and shaped the lip.

PUSH UP

Also called kick up. Describes the hummock formed in the base of a bottle. The original purpose was to make the bottle stand.

SALT GLAZE

Used on most pottery bottles and jugs. The glaze is formed by throwing salt into the kiln when it reaches the maximum temperature.

SEAM

Surface mark on a container blown in a mold or made in an automatic bottle machine.

SNAP CASE

A mechanical device invented about 1850 which was used to hold a bottle in place for finishing. Free blown or mold blown bottles held in a snap case do not have a pontil scar.

SUCTION MACHINE CUT-OFF SCAR

A well defined circular valve mark on the base of automatic machine made bottles.

SUNCAST AMETHYST

From the late 1800's to 1915 manganese oxide was used in the manufacturer of clear glass. It is the presence of this chemical that causes clear glass to turn amethyst when exposed to sunlight.

SUNCAST YELLOW OR STRAW

Glass which has turned from clear to pale yellow by exposure to sunlight. Selenium was the oxide used in the manufacture of clear glass from 1916 to 1930.

WHITTLE MARKS

A term used to describe the dimpled, hammered or wavy appearance of some glass containers. This effect was caused during mold blowing when molten glass was placed in a cold metal mold.

Acknowledgements

To compile our price guides information and photographs are obtained from many sources; in fact, without outside help these books would not exist. It is not possible to mention every source of this data, however the following have given us generous co-operation and we would like them to know that their help has given us the means to complete this book.

Sincere thanks to you all.

Ron Armstrong
Lindsay, Ontario

Allan Bowes
Kingston, Ontario

Margo Sparrow
Brewers Association of Canada
Ottawa, Ontario

Billie Lawrence formerly of
Cameron School House
Cameron, Ontario

Jim & Marg Caswell
Cas's Collectables
Newcastle, Ontario

Coca-Cola Company
Atlanta, Georgia

Alan Turner
Crush Canada Inc.
Don Mills, Ontario

Donna & Gerald English
Peterborough, Ontario

Carl Doughty
Peterborough, Ontario

Carl Fox
Ottawa, Ontario

Members of Limestone Chapter and the
Golden Horseshoe Chapter of The
Canadian Brewerianists

Vern & Barb Haynes
Bath, Ontario

Paula (M.D.) Pearson
London, Ontario

Harry Presser
Ottawa, Ontario

Raymond Sams
Sam's Collectables
Bath, Ontario

Lawrence C. Sherk
Toronto, Ontario

Shirley & Gordon Shorter
Ottawa, Ontario

J. Kevin Meens
Sleeman Brewing & Malting Co. Ltd.

Fred Spoestra
Fonthill, Ontario

Barry Townsend
Port Perry, Ontario

Marg & Bob Walker
Richmond, Ontario

Joyce Blyth
Guelph, Ontario

Scott Jordan
Ottawa, Ontario

Robin Newton-Smith
Cambridge, Ontario

Bert Spring
Haliburton, Ontario

Bibliography

BARCLAY, John C. "The Canadian Fruit Jar Report"
The Author. 1977.
"The Canadian Fruit Jar Report" Book 2. The Author. 1986, 1987.

BIRD, Douglas & Marion and Charles Corke. "A Century of Antique Glass Fruit Jars"
The Authors. 1971.

BOWERING, Ian. "The Art & Mystery of Brewing in Ontario" General Store Publishing House Inc. 1988.

BREWERS Association of Canada.
"Annual Statistical Bulletin" 1988
"Brewing in Canada" 1965.
"The Brewing Industry in Canada in 1988"

CARTER, Morris and Jim Hostetler. "Ontario Soda Water Bottles"
The Authors. 1975.

COCA-COLA Company. "The Chronicle of Coca-Cola Since 1886"

CHOPPING, George. "Bottles of the Canadian Prairies"
The Author. 1978.

DONALDSON, Gerald and Gerald Lampert. "The Great Canadian Beer Book" McClelland and Stewart Limited. 1975.

HARRIS, W.F. "Nova Scotia Pops and Crocks" The Author. 1977.

HASTIN, Bud & Vickie. "Avon Bottle Encyclopedia" The Authors. 1980.

HERR, J.A. "The Ontario Soda Water Bottle Collectors Index and Price Guide." The Author.

HILL, Deborah Goldstein. "Price Guide to Coca-Cola Collectibles" Wallace Homestead. 1984.

KONAROWSKI, John A. "What Happened to our Milk Man?" The Author. 1985.

PETRETTI, Allan. "Petretti's Coca-Cola Collectibles Price Guide" Nostalgia Publication Inc. 1989.

PHILLIPS, Glen C. "The Ontario Soda Water Manufacturers and Brewers Gazetteer and Business Directory" Clearwater Publishing Company. 1987.

SHERK, Lawrence C. and Martin Wray. "The Canadian Brewerianist Beer Tray Inventory" The Authors. 1989.

TOULOUSE, Julian H. "A Collector's Manual - Fruit Jars" Thomas Nelson and Sons. 1969.

UNITT, Doris & Peter. "Bottles in Canada" Clock House Publications 1972.
"Unitt's Across Canada Bottle Price Guide" Clock House Publications. 1981.

UNITT, Peter and Anne Worrall. "Unitt's Bottle Book & Price Guide" Clock House Publications. 1985.

URQUHART, O. "Bottlers and Bottles Canadian" The Author. 1976.

VIENNEAU, Azor. "The Bottle Collector." Petheric Press. 1971.

Peter Sutton–Smith studied architecture and land surveying before his army service with the Royal Engineers, where he served with the Army of Occupation in Austria. Upon demobilization, he started a new career in social work, and graduated from the University of Leicester, England.

Peter Sutton–Smith came to Canada in 1969 to take up a social work appointment in the Province of Quebec. He is now a member of the Ontario College of Social Workers, and holds both Canadian and British citizenship.

A man with a passionate love of antiques, Peter Sutton–Smith opened an antique shop in partnership with his wife in 1975. They specialized in English and European antiques, with a bias towards early porcelains, 18th & l9th century copper and brass, and period furniture.

Appointed Editorial Director of the *Antique Showcase* editorial board in 1982, he became owner and publisher of the magazine and *Ontario Directory of Antique Shops* eighteen months later. He has often given talks on antiques, is the author of several published articles on the subject, and has been involved in the establishment of several important antique shows. He, with his wife, now compile the *"Unitts" Canadian Price Guides on Antiques*, and is revising several past publications.

Barbara Sutton–Smith, has been a full time antiques dealer for over 21 years, but she has been involved in the field for most of her life. Her specialty is early English and European porcelains, and although her interests sparked many academic studies gaining her much knowledge she believes "knowledge and practical experience are the basics for the making of an expert."

Before coming to Canada, Barbara Sutton–Smith taught high school social studies and was involved periodically in residential social work.

She has received a literary award for her fiction, and has appeared several times on local television in her capacity as an antiques expert and enthusiast. Her articles have appeared in a number of publications.

For the past fifteen years Barbara Sutton–Smith has been the Editorial Director of *Antique Showcase*, Canada's only national antiques magazine, now in its 35th year of continuous publication.

Index